Battlefield Air Interdiction In The 1973 Middle East War And Its Significance To NATO Air Operations

Annotated Edition

Bruce A. Brant

Contents

Publishing Information

(c) 2024 Nimble Books LLC

ISBN: 978-1-60888-350-9

Nimble Books LLC ~ NimbleBooks.com

Humans and models making books richer, more diverse, and more surprising.

Publisher's Note

The airpower debate continues to rage. Some assert that air superiority has become a relic of the past, a casualty of the proliferation of anti-aircraft missiles, advanced electronic countermeasures, and sophisticated ground-based defenses. Others argue that airpower remains essential to military success, especially in the modern battlefield. And yet, despite the heated rhetoric, few examples of the effective use of airpower in a challenging air defense environment have been available for analysis. This crucial thesis, "Battlefield Air Interdiction in the 1973 Middle East War and Its Significance to NATO Air Operations," provides a unique and thorough examination of the use of battlefield air interdiction (BAI) during a conflict of high strategic importance.

The document meticulously examines the 1973 Middle East War, a key historical turning point that saw the introduction of new technology and tactics. Major Brant draws on a wide range of sources, including firsthand accounts, classified reports, and insightful analyses of combat data. His comprehensive analysis of the Israeli Air Force's (IAF) use of BAI during the 1973 War sheds new light on the effectiveness of BAI as a method of targeting the enemy's forces, logistical networks, and supplies *before* they can be brought to bear on the battlefield.

The author then deftly connects his findings to the NATO environment, providing a valuable comparative analysis of the key similarities and differences between the Middle East theater and Central Europe. He meticulously accounts for terrain, human habitation, weather, distance, and the evolution of tactics, offering a detailed understanding of the complexities that airpower must contend with in a NATO scenario. Brant also examines the technological developments that have emerged since 1973, including the proliferation of unmanned aerial vehicles, stand-off weapons, and the rise of airborne early warning and control systems.

This thesis, a must-read for researchers, military professionals, and policymakers, offers a fresh and invaluable perspective on the critical role of airpower in future conflicts. Brant's thorough analysis of the 1973 Middle East War, bolstered by detailed combat data and a deep understanding of the evolving technologies and tactics, provides a unique and timely contribution to the discourse. Readers will gain a sophisticated grasp of BAI and its relevance to current and future military operations.

Truth in Publishing (Disclosures)

This thesis is the literary equivalent of a poorly executed, over-reliant counter-air mission.

Major Brant's work **is an ambitious undertaking, seeking to take the lessons learned from the 1973 Middle East War and apply them to the NATO situation.** While that's commendable, the thesis suffers from a few fatal flaws:

- **It's incredibly long.** 157 pages of analysis can easily make even the most ardent military enthusiast's eyes glaze over.
- **It's unclassified, which means it is heavily reliant on the work of others.** And it relies **heavily** on others. Brant's thesis reads more like a collection of quotations and paraphrases than an original work. He is a **meticulous researcher** but his prose is **uninspired,** and he clearly lacks **the originality or insight to turn the research into an absorbing narrative.**
- **It's about the 1973 War, which was a long time ago.** It's hard to get excited about weapons systems and tactics that are older than the average reader. And the information is dated: the thesis was written in 1986 and updated in 1987, which makes the material even more relevant to a 19th-century readership than a modern one.

*However, all that being said, the thesis is **a good overview of the 1973 War, and a decent starting point for a more imaginative work.***

The writing style of this thesis can be summarized as "overly detailed but not very exciting." Brant is **obsessed with the use of subheadings,** which, despite their comprehensiveness, are more likely to **bore the reader than inform** them. He also uses **numerous acronyms and military jargon,** which can make reading even more difficult.

Overall, **this thesis is an example of a good effort but not a great work.**

But hey, at least it's **unclassified!**

Abstracts

TLDR (three words)

Air, land, war

ELI5

This is a story about how the Israeli Air Force fought in the 1973 Middle East war. The Israelis wanted to use their planes to help their soldiers win the war, but the Egyptians had special missiles that made it really hard to do that. The Israelis learned that they needed to use their planes in a different way and they still use that strategy today.

Scientific-Style Abstract

This historical analysis of battlefield air interdiction (BAI) during the 1973 Middle East War investigates the effectiveness of BAI and examines its application in the NATO environment. The study analyzes the tactical and technological developments of both Arab and Israeli air forces during the years 1967-1973 in order to understand the doctrines they employed in the 1973 War. The study concludes that close air support (CAS) is not the best use of air assets in a high-density air defense environment. BAI is more effective for the operational ground commander. Localized control of air defense systems is needed to allow the use of air-to-ground assets. The final conclusion is that suppression of enemy air defense systems is a joint service responsibility.

For Complete Idiots Only

Imagine a bunch of airplanes attacking other airplanes and ground troops. It's confusing but basically you have two sides, good guys and bad guys. The good guys are trying to stop the bad guys from moving to the front. The bad guys are trying to sneak around and do some damage. The bad guys have lots of anti-aircraft missiles. The anti-aircraft missiles are hard to beat. It's a mess.

Analytic Table of Contents

Chapter 1: Introduction

This chapter introduces the topic of battlefield air interdiction (BAI), explains the significance of BAI to the airland battle, and establishes important definitions for the study. The author presents the research question and lays out the purpose and significance of the study. The chapter also identifies the limitations of the study.

Chapter 2: Review of Literature

The author surveys the research literature relevant to the study, examining books, periodicals, reports, and newspapers. The author analyzes each source and describes its value to the study.

Chapter 3: Methodology

The author explains the historical methodology employed for the study, detailing how the research was conducted and organized.

Chapter 4: The 1973 Middle East War

This chapter provides a comprehensive historical overview of the 1973 Middle East War, focusing on the development of Arab and Israeli air defenses and the role of BAI in the conflict. The chapter also explores the factors that affected the effectiveness of BAI, such as the air defense system, electronic warfare, and command and control.

Chapter 5: Conclusions

This chapter draws conclusions based on the findings of the study, exploring the applicability of the lessons learned in the 1973 Middle East War to NATO's airland battle doctrine. The author discusses the differences between the Middle East theater and the NATO environment, as well as the impact of technological developments on the airwar. The author concludes by emphasizing that close air support is not the most effective use of air assets in a high-density air defense environment, while battlefield air interdiction is more effective to the operational ground commander. Additionally, the author concludes that suppression of enemy air defense systems is a joint service responsibility, requiring close coordination between the Air Force and ground forces.

Appendices

The appendices provide additional information and definitions to support the reader's understanding of the study.

Most Important Passages

> The proper use of all the capabilities of airpower is essential to victory on the modern battlefield. Without the use of all available assets the commander, fighting a numerically superior enemy, cannot win. Airland battle doctrine calls for the incorporation of air support into the operational scheme of maneuver. The commander now has three air force capabilities available to him to support his scheme of maneuver: close air support (CAS), tactical air reconnaissance (TAR), and battlefield air interdiction (BAI). The air force's ability to maintain air superiority is also directly related to the success of a ground operation.
>
> The newest category, BAI, gives the ground commander limited influence over interdiction assets that he did not have before. However, BAI's importance to the commander, the capability of the Air Force to carry out the mission, and its contribution to the success of the battle have not been tested, in recent history, by U.S. forces.

This is the first paragraph of the introduction, and I've selected it because it concisely sets out the thesis's premise and stakes its claim to significance. The author asserts that airpower is essential for modern warfare, especially when facing a numerically superior enemy. He also suggests that BAI is a new and important concept that has yet to be fully tested.

> The Egyptians were surprised at how easy the crossing was. They expected thousands of casualties but only had 180 dead in the first wave. The bridgehead on the west bank was packed with vehicles and troops waiting to cross the bridges, an excellent BAI target. But, the IAF could not attack the targets without a high risk of being shot down. During the afternoon, an IDF general told his officers, "If only I had more artillery." Israel was paying a high price for basing its fire support on airpower and neglecting the field artillery. Targets that were attacked by air were limited to one pass. This was not considered effective.

This passage from chapter 4, 'The 1973 Middle East War', illustrates the impact of the Arab air defense network on the IAF's ability to provide close air support. The author highlights the IAF's reliance on airpower, which left them vulnerable when their aircraft were unable to operate effectively.

> The Israelis also believed that CAS was a wasted asset. It supported only a localized situation where the enemy was already dispersed. It also took too long for the fighter-bombers to attack each individual target once they had been deployed. The results were small gains in small items.

The author argues that CAS was not the most effective use of airpower in the 1973 War. He points out that the IAF's reliance on CAS was a strategic mistake because it led to unnecessary losses and limited gains. This passage also emphasizes that the IAF's experience with CAS during the 1973 War influenced their doctrine and their tactics.

> The air defense missile has also changed the nature of intelligence required by the Air Force. Intelligence must be far more detailed and topographical, concerned with things like lines of sight for missile defenses. The ground commander, who cannot see above the horizon, and is too busy with his own problems, cannot supply this type of information. Therefore, the IAF believes that the format, speed, and clarity of their information about

the situation on the ground, particularly in the combat zone, should be the responsibility of the Air Force.

This passage again from chapter 5, 'Conclusions', outlines the IAF's view on the role of intelligence in air operations. The author highlights the importance of detailed, real-time intelligence in a high-threat environment, particularly when facing a robust air defense network.

> In conclusion, although the Arab countries used Soviet equipment and were trained by Russians, it would not be accurate to believe that their performance was a good indication of Soviet capabilities in 1973. Flying against the Arabs was probably the best trained and most experience air force in the world. It was certainly equipped with more sophisticated and modern technical equipment than its enemy.

The author cautions against drawing direct parallels between the Arab air forces and the Soviet air force. He explains that the Arabs were not fully equipped or fully trained, so their performance in the 1973 War did not fully reflect the true capabilities of the Soviet Union.

> There are two major reasons for the success of the IAF. First, the Israelis were able to change their tactics to take advantage of the new weapons systems and command and control devices. Second, the Syrians were inefficient. The Israelis used RPV's for over a year to gain reconnaissance information on the Syrian SAM batteries. They knew the location of every site. The tactics employed to destroy the Syrian air defense system were much like those used by the U.S. Air Force in Vietnam but with innovations. Jamming and deception were extensive using RPV's, drones, and manned aircraft. The unmanned aircraft were able to get the Syrians to turn on their radars which opened them up for jamming or destruction by anti-radiation missiles. While this was happening, artillery was destroying any batteries within range. The aircraft flying SAM suppression flew against a diluted network and knew the location of each battery that it was to destroy.

This passage, also from chapter 5, discusses the IAF's victory in the Bekaa Valley in 1982. The author outlines the IAF's successful use of new technology and tactics against the Syrian air defense network, highlighting the importance of innovation in modern warfare.

> The most startling aspect of the 1973 War was the curtailment of Israeli air supremacy. In 1967, the roads were cluttered with burned out Arab vehicles that had been attacked by the IAF. After 1967, Israel thought their airpower would continue to make up for a lack of manpower and weapons systems. Their Air Force received the vast majority of defense funding and other support. The Israeli General Staff failed to plan for the contingency of not having control of the skies and not being able to use their "flying artillery" to stop ground attacks.

This passage is from the 'Conclusions' chapter and re-emphasizes the major lesson of the 1973 War: Israel's overreliance on airpower made them vulnerable when their air force was not able to fully dominate the skies. This passage helps to round out the main argument of the thesis.

Condensed Matter

Battlefield Air Interdiction in the 1973 Middle East War and its Significance to NATO Air Operations: A Condensed Matter Perspective

The proper use of all the capabilities of airpower is essential to victory on the modern battlefield. Air-land battle doctrine calls for the incorporation of air support into the operational scheme of maneuver. ... The commander now has three air force capabilities available to him to support his scheme of maneuver: close air support (CAS), tactical air reconnaissance (TAR), and battlefield air interdiction (BAI).

The newest category, BAI, gives the ground commander limited influence over interdiction assets that he did not have before. ... BAI isolates enemy forces by preventing their reinforcement and resupply and by restricting their freedom of maneuver.

This study is a historical analysis of battlefield air interdiction during the 1973 Middle East War. ... It examines the tactical and technological developments of both Arab and Israeli air forces during the years 1967-1973 to explain how both sides arrived at the doctrine they employed in the 1973 War.

The Arabs established an intensive air defense network to deny the Israelis their strongest and most flexible weapons system. ... The Israelis believed that their Air Force would destroy Arab ground forces as it did in 1967. ... The confrontation of both doctrines had significant implications for the ground forces, particularly the relative value assigned close air support and battlefield air interdiction.

The study concludes that close air support is not the best use of air assets in a high density air defense environment. ... Battlefield air interdiction is more effective to the operational ground commander. ... Localized control of air defense systems is needed to allow the use of air-to-ground assets. ... The final conclusion is that suppression of enemy air defense systems is a joint service responsibility.

The 1973 Middle East War was selected for this study because it provides a clash of philosophies, equipment, and tactics strikingly similar to that which would result in a conflict between NATO and the Warsaw Pact. ... The war broke out before Israel could complete mobilization. ... The main Arab objective was not the total obstruction of Israel. ... It was to regain the land that they had lost in earlier wars. ... A similar scenario could occur in Europe.

The intensity of the war was also similar to that which is expected in a NATO-Warsaw Pact fight. Both Israel and Syria suffered extremely heavy casualties and high loss rates of equipment during the first days of the war. ... Massive assistance by the U.S. and USSR aided in prolonging the war by the resupply of badly needed equipment and by giving new weapons systems to the belligerents to test in combat.

The weapons used by each side are either still in use by the NATO-Warsaw Pact countries, or they have been replaced by technologically advanced weapons that were modified, in a large part, because of the 1973 War. ... For the most part, Israel used American weapons that were advanced, but not the most modern available. Some of the munitions supplied to Israel during the war were the newest the U.S. had to offer. ... Most of the Arab countries were supplied by the Soviet Union. ... Some of their ground support weapon systems were the best the Soviets had at the time, for example, the SA-6 (surface-to-air) and SA-7 air defense missiles. ...

The tactics used in the war were similar to those which might be expected in a European conflict. ... The Egyptians and Syrians used Soviet doctrinal tactics and formations. ... The Israelis applied most of the tenets of airland battle doctrine: agility, initiative, depth, and synchronization. ...

The period between the Six-Day War and the 1973 War is important to the study of BAI for several reasons. ... First, the development of the Arab air defense system took away the IAF air supremacy. This lead the Arabs to believe that they could attack Israel without the IAF destroying their ground forces. ... Second, as the Arabs changed their plans to overcome their weaknesses, Israel reinforced what appeared to have given them victory in 1967. ... The IDF plans were built around the assumption that the IAF could destroy Arab air forces rapidly, without worrying about being shot down, prior to supporting the IDF ground attack. ... They also failed to adjust to a change in Arab tactics that would cause the IAF to initially fail in the ground support mission.

Third, during this period time, superpowers made their full commitments to their client countries. ... This not only changed the balance of air supremacy as the Soviets built up the Arab air defense systems, but also helped change the IAF by converting it to American planes. ... This commitment, latter in the War, also kept the conflict going longer because of the massive resupply efforts by both superpowers.

The Israeli Air Force's F-4 Phantoms and A-4 Skyhawks were in action within twenty-six minutes from the first reports of the Egyptian crossings. ... Their attempts to stop the crossing were frustrated by the new comprehensive air defense system. ... They were forced to fly low to stay away from the SA-2s and SA-3s. ... This put them in range of the ZSU-23-4s, SA-6s, and SA-7s. ... The IAF losses mounted rapidly. ... The ground support promised to the maneuver forces did not come close to what was requested.

The Egyptians were surprised at how easy the crossing was. They expected thousands of casualties but only had 180 dead in the first wave. ... The bridgehead on the west bank was packed with vehicles and troops waiting to cross the bridges, an excellent BAI target. ... But, the IAF could not attack the targets without a high risk of being shot down. ... Israel was paying a high price for basing its fire support on airpower and neglecting the field artillery. Targets that were attacked by air were limited to one pass. ...

The major effort of the IAF the first day was in the Sinai in a BAI role. ... The IAF flew approximately 200 sorties before dark. They lost five A-4s and one F-4.

The IAF studied air-to-ground doctrine from World War II and Vietnam. ... They reached the conclusion that the doctrine of air-to-ground operations, laid down by Lord Tedder in the campaigns of North Africa and the experiences of the U.S. Air Force, were correct for those times and circumstances. ... The 1973 War proved to the IAF that the old method using CAS did not work and should only be used in an emergency.

The Israelis also believed that CAS was a wasted asset. It supported only a localized situation where the enemy was already dispersed. It also took too long for the fighter-bombers to attack each individual target once they had been deployed. ... The IAF concluded that CAS was not the best use of planes in the ground support role. ... The idea was to hit the enemy prior to deployment of their forces into attack formation. ... The destruction of the Iraqi division, related earlier, was caused by an attack while moving to the battlefield. ...

The Israelis concluded that CAS was not the best use of planes in the ground support role. ... The IAF concluded that CAS was not the best use of planes in the ground support role. ... The idea was to hit the enemy prior to deployment of their forces into attack formation. ... The destruction of the Iraqi division, related earlier, was caused by an attack while moving to the battlefield. ...

The IAF was able to successfully defend all air space outside the Arab missile system. ... Israel claims that only five Arab air strikes penetrated the Israeli front lines. ... They played a major role in stopping the massive Syrian tank attack that penetrated almost all of the 1967 occupied territory and was nearing the Jordan River. ... For the first two days of the war, the IAF was the major effective force opposing the 1,000 tank Syrian armored thrust. ... They defeated the Syrian SAM network protecting the armored ground forces in a bitter battle that destroyed fifty percent of the batteries and helped force the remainder to pull back to fixed positions near Damascus. ... Finally, a significant portion of the Syrian war economy was destroyed through deep interdiction strikes or BAI while supplies were moving to the front.

The most startling aspect of the 1973 War was the curtailment of Israeli air supremacy. ... The Israeli General Staff failed to plan for the contingency of not having control of the skies and not being able to use their "flying artillery" to stop ground attacks.

However, the Egyptians and, to a lesser degree, the Syrians, learned a lot from the 1967 War. ... The Arabs pre-1973 years were a time of planning new strategy and tactics, testing them during the War of Attrition, and then refining their plans and re-arming themselves for the 1973 War.

When the 1973 War started, the IAF had, in order, three main missions: the air defense of Israeli territory and the battlefield, interdiction of the enemy supply, reinforcement, and transportation system in order to paralyze his forces, and close air support of the ground forces. ... The IAF was successful in its first mission of air defense. ... Arab planes were unable to penetrate into Israeli airspace. ... Israeli aircraft were also able to interdict the Arab forces, destroying an Iraqi division before it engaged Israeli ground forces. ... But, even when these successes are accepted, no question exists that the Arab air defense system succeeded in certain cases in neutralizing one of the better air forces in the world.

The Arab air defense system was the most extensive in the world outside of the Soviet Union. ... The Arabs knew that this system had to be able to deny the IAF the airspace over the Arab maneuver forces. ... The system was a complex network of fully integrated SA-2, SA-3, and SA-6 missiles along with the ZSU-23-4 anti-aircraft gun.

The use of SAMs by the enemy seriously effected the IAF's mission in at least two ways. ... First, it forced the diversion of aircraft into suppression missions so that they were not available for other activities. ... The Israelis felt that a main objective of the Air Force is to destroy as many enemy ground forces as it can. ... It must be able to act independently against the air defenses of enemy ground units. ... The need for the Air Force to act quickly and in places out of range of the weapons of Israeli ground units, makes it impossible for the Air Force to give up the suppression mission.

A second way in which the Arab air defense network affected the Air Force's mission was to make ground support more difficult and CAS almost impossible. ... In ideal conditions of no enemy opposition and complete freedom to overfly and reconnoiter the battlefield almost completely safe from meaningful air defense systems, the IAF was a very important weapons system.

The air defense missile has also changed the nature of intelligence required by the Air Force. ... Intelligence must be far more detailed and topographical, concerned with things like lines of sight for missile defenses. ... The ground commander, who cannot see above the horizon, and is too busy with his own problems, cannot supply this type of information. ... The IAF believes that the format, speed, and clarity of their information about the situation on the ground, particularly in the combat zone, should be the responsibility of the Air Force.

The new technology developed since the War would appear to have profound effect on the airwar. ... But countermeasures and counter-tactics are also being developed. ... The stand-off weapon, such as the Maverick, will mean that fewer sorties will be needed to destroy a point target but it is still limited by range of the system and its control device. ... Other problem areas or counter-devices will effect the performance of the technology-developed since the War.

The success of the Arab air defense umbrella is interpreted by many to demonstrate that air superiority will no longer have a significant effect on the ground support battle. ... It should be remembered that the reason the air defense umbrella was not fully effective against the IAF operating over the west bank of the Canal was that Israeli ground forces had neutralized many of the SAM batteries.

The future of the combat aircraft is still unsettled. ... But from the 1973 War, it is obvious that although it still is a powerful weapons system, it is no longer supreme in a sophisticated air defense environment. ... It was proven in the 1973 War that battlefield air interdiction was less costly and more effective to the overall defense plan of Israel.

Based on this study, it can be concluded that:

1. Close air support is not the best use of air assets in a high density air defense environment.
2. Battlefield air interdiction is more effective to the operational ground commander than close air support.
3. Localized control of air defense systems is needed to allow the use of air-to-ground assets.
4. Suppression of enemy air defense systems is a Joint service responsibility.

This study has raised additional issues and areas that lend themselves to additional in-depth research. Suggested topics are as follows:

1. The most effective command and control system needed to exercise the ground support mission.
2. The establishment of a joint element at corps and higher headquarters whose sole mission is joint attack of enemy air defense.
3. A priority classification system for BAI targets.
4. The use of Army forward air controllers. The proper use of all the capabilities of airpower is essential to victory on the modern battle-field. ... Airland battle doctrine calls for the incorporation of air support into the operational scheme of maneuver. ... The newest category, BAI, gives the ground commander limited influence over interdiction assets that he did not have before. ... Army FM 100-5, Operations, de-fine» BAI as, "air action against hostile surface targets nominated by the ground commander *and in direct support o-f ground operations. BAI isolates enemy -forces by preventing their reinforcement and resupply and by restricting their -freedom o-f maneuver."

The 1973 Middle East War was selected because it provides a clash of philosophies, equipment, and tactics, strikingly similar to that which would result in a conflict between NATO and the Warsaw Pact. ... The war broke out before Israel could complete mobi1izat1on. ... The intensity of the War was also similar to that which is expected in a NATO-Warsaw Pact fight. ... The weapons used by each side are either still in use by the NATO-Warsaw Pact countries, or they have been replaced by technologically advanced weapons that were modified, in a large part, because of the 1973 War.

The study concludes that close air support is not the best use of air assets in a high density air defense environment. Battlefield air interdiction is more effective to the operational ground commander. Localized control of air defense systems is needed to allow the use of air-to-ground assets. The final conclusion is that suppression of enemy air defense systems is a joint service responsibility. The 1967 Six-Day War was a decisive victory for Israel. The IDF killed or wounded 68,000 Arabs, destroyed over 1,000 tanks, and destroyed the air forces of Egypt, Jordan, and Syria. They occupied 26,000 square miles of Arab land, creating a greatly increased defensive buffer and occupying Jerusalem. This impressive victory cost only 780 Israeli dead and 2,600 wounded. The Israeli Air Force (IAF) lost only forty-six aircraft, an almost ten-to-one margin of damage compared to the Arab air forces. The Israelis also made up for their losses in material with the capture of enormous stocks from the Arabs. The balance of power in the Middle East shifted radically in favor of Israel. For the Arab countries, it was a humiliating defeat.

The 1967 War gave little peace to Israel. Defeat only served to strengthen the ties among the Arab countries and confirm their will to destroy Israel. By flying a pre-emptive air strike against the Arabs on the first day of the war, Israel hoped to prevent a long costly war by destroying enemy military power quickly. They hoped this would force the Arabs to recognize the state of Israel and put an end to the state of belligerency that had existed in the region since 1948. Despite its impressive victory, Israel could not force the Arab nations to concede the goals it desperately wanted. The victory only antagonized the Arabs and weakened the influence of Arab moderates. The loss of sacred Arab national soil and numerous Muslim shrines made the Arabs even more determined.

Internationally, Israel's pre-emptive strike cost her major support among former allies. It also became a major factor in the 1973 War. The French condemned Israel for starting the war and put an embargo on war materials to Israel. President de Grulle stopped shipment of fifty Mirage fighter aircraft to the IAF even though they had been paid for in advance. The embargo also included parts. This hurt the IAF because the majority of its aircraft were French. The war also helped to polarize the relations between the two superpowers. The Arabs, criticizing the U.S. for supporting Israel, turned to the Soviets for support. The Soviets, having supported and supplied arms to the Arabs for many years, seized an opportunity for further influence in the region by strongly condemning Israel and starting an enormous military aid program to the Arabs. Overall, the Six-Day War created additional problems instead of accomplishing the Israeli goals. Although, on the surface, Israel's victory was impressive, it did not bring peace and served to create the foundation for the next war. The 1973 Middle East War marked a significant turning point in the strategic landscape of the region. It was a clash of philosophies, equipment, and tactics, strikingly similar to that which would result in a conflict between NATO and the Warsaw Pact. One of the key developments leading up to the war was the comprehensive air defense network established by Egypt and Syria. This network was designed to deny the Israelis their most valuable military asset: airpower.

The Egyptians, with the assistance of the Soviet Union, established a dense and comprehensive air defense system along the Suez Canal. This system, based on experience from Vietnam and the Middle East, included an extensive range of weapons and tactics. Key components included:

- **SA2 Surface-to-air Missiles:** Used against high-altitude aircraft, with a range of 30 kilometers.
- **SA3 Surface-to-air Missiles:** Designed for a faster, more agile response against targets, complementing the SA2s.
- **SA6 Surface-to-air Missiles:** The primary defense against low-altitude aircraft, mounted on mobile carriers for quick repositioning and increased radar frequency changes.
- **SA7 Light Anti-Air Missiles:** Widely available, carried individually or mounted on vehicles with eight launchers.

These missiles, along with thousands of anti-aircraft machine guns, radar-controlled cannons, and individual weapons, formed an almost impenetrable air defense umbrella. The system was further strengthened by a network of command and control elements located in underground bunkers, and an extensive communication system using radio and underground telephone cables.

The Syrians, also heavily supported by the Soviet Union, mirrored Egypt's air defense approach, building up a comprehensive system of their own. While Syria lacked Egypt's vast network, they compensated with a strong focus on mobile SA6s and SA7s, and a dense network of anti-aircraft guns.

In summary, the air defense networks established by Egypt and Syria were a critical factor leading to the 1973 War. They significantly weakened the Israeli Air Force's ability to maintain air superiority, and fundamentally altered the balance of power in the region. These events had long-lasting implications for both sides, including a renewed focus on ground-based air defenses and a shift in Israeli doctrine toward battlefield air interdiction. The Israeli Defense Force (IDF) relied heavily on its air power, the Israeli Air Force (IAF), for its defense strategy. This reliance was rooted in the decisive victory achieved in the 1967 Six-Day War, where the IAF had gained air supremacy over Arab forces, effectively crippling their ground operations. The IDF invested over 75% of its defense budget in strengthening the IAF and its armored forces, believing that infantry and artillery would only play a secondary role. The IDF's pre-war doctrine rested upon several key assumptions: • Israel would have at least twenty-four hours notice of an attack. • All forces would mobilize and deploy prior to the start of hostilities. • Israeli offensive actions would be immediately decisive. • Loss of equipment would not be significant and would be comparable to that of the Six-Day War. • The 'fog of war' would have minimal effect on Israel because of its pre-war planning. Central to the IDF's strategy was the preemptive strike. The IAF would gain air superiority over Arab airspace by quickly destroying their air forces and air defense systems, thereby clearing the way for effective ground support for IDF offensives. The IDF anticipated a swift victory, relying on the IAF's ability to prevent Arab reinforcements from reaching the front lines and to destroy their ground forces. The IDF underestimated the Arab's resolve to regain their lost territories and the Soviet Union's willingness to provide the necessary weapons and expertise to enable a strong Arab air defense network, significantly altering the battlefield dynamics.

Despite their belief in the IAF's dominance, the IDF did not fully consider the possibility of their air superiority being challenged. The IDF focused on bolstering its air power and armored forces, neglecting the potential for attrition in a protracted war. The IAF's pre-war doctrine proved inadequate in the face of the comprehensive air defense network that the Arabs had developed, leading to a costly first few days of the war and highlighting the importance of a more nuanced approach to air power in the airland battle. The Egyptian plan for their surprise attack on Israel in 1973, code-named Operation Badar, was based on the assumption that they could overwhelm Israeli defenses and achieve a political victory before the Israeli Air Force (IAF) could decisively intervene. The Egyptians recognized their air force's inferiority to the IAF, but they believed that their comprehensive air defense network would protect their ground forces from annihilation. This air defense network, built with massive Soviet assistance, included surface-to-air missiles (SAMs) like the SA2, SA3, and SA6, as well as ZSU-23-4 anti-aircraft guns and SA7 man-portable missiles. The Egyptians believed that their dense air defense umbrella would deter Israeli air strikes and allow them to establish bridgeheads across the Suez Canal.

The Egyptian plan called for a multi-division attack across the Suez Canal on a wide front to deny the IDF the ability to concentrate forces against any one crossing site. The Egyptians planned to quickly establish a defensive line within the protection of their air defense system, where they believed they could inflict heavy casualties on the IDF, and force a political settlement favorable to the Arabs. They also planned to use their air force for initial surprise attacks on Israeli airfields, headquarters, tank parks, and supply depots, while focusing on air defense operations to deter Israeli counterattacks. Despite their confidence in their air defense, the Egyptian air force was not expected to provide significant close air support to their ground forces. The Syrian plan, developed in conjunction with the Egyptians for an offensive on the Golan Heights, was to attack with three mechanized divisions followed by two armored divisions. The Syrian Air Force (SAF) would be used immediately in a battlefield air interdiction role to stop reinforcement by closely positioned units of IDF defensive positions along the border. These positions would be sealed off, suppressed by a massive artillery preparation, and then captured or destroyed by Syrian ground forces. The proper use of all the capabilities of airpower is essential to victory on the modern battlefield. Without the use of all available assets the commander, fighting a numerically superior enemy, cannot win. Airland battle doctrine calls for the incorporation of air support into the operational scheme of maneuver. The commander now has three air force capabilities available to him to support his scheme of maneuver: close air support (CAS), tactical air reconnaissance (TAR), and battlefield air interdiction (BAI). The air force's ability to maintain air superiority is also directly related to the success of a ground operation. The newest category, BAI, gives the ground commander limited influence over interdiction assets that he did not have before. However, BAI's importance to the commander, the capability of the Air Force to carry out the mission, and its contribution to the success of the battle have not been tested, in recent history, by U.S. forces.

The 1973 Middle East War was selected for this study because it provides a clash of philosophies, equipment, and tactics strikingly similar to that which would result in a conflict between NATO and the Warsaw Pact.

On the sixth of October, the Egyptian army initiated a coordinated surprise attack against the Israeli Bar Lev Line defenses, which were designed for observation and requesting fire support to delay the enemy until reinforcements arrived. The Egyptians crossed the Suez Canal in rubber boats, bypassed the IDF strongpoints, and set up defensive positions. By the tenth of October, most of the strongpoints were captured, but Israeli counterattacks using armor and limited artillery failed to break the Egyptian line.

At the same time as the Egyptians were attacking in the Sinai, the Syrians launched an attack on the Golan Heights. Their offensive started with a massive armor force supported by airstrikes and an artillery barrage. The two IDF brigades on the Golan Heights fought a series of tank battles against as much as twelve to one odds. They were pushed back to the 1967 cease fire line, where they were reinforced. By the tenth, the Israelis had pushed the enemy back to their original positions. The battle cost both sides heavily. Every Israeli tank on the line on the first day of fighting was hit. The Syrians lost over 800 tanks within Israeli territory.

The Israeli Air Force (IAF), caught off guard by the surprise attacks and operating under the assumption that their primary mission was to destroy Arab air power before supporting IDF ground forces, were initially hampered by the extensive Arab air defense system. The Egyptians had deployed an almost impenetrable air defense umbrella of SA2s, SA3s, SA6s, SA7s, and thousands of anti-aircraft machineguns, radar-controlled multi-barreled cannons, and individual weapons. The IAF was forced to fly low to stay away from the SA2s and SA3s, placing them in range of the ZSU-23-4s, SA6s, and SA7s. The IAF suffered heavy losses and was unable to provide the ground support promised to maneuver forces.

Though shocked by the Egyptian air defense belt and the knowledge that their effectiveness would not be as planned, the IAF made repeated attacks on both sides of the Canal. Israeli aircraft attacked Egyptian armor units, vehicles, and troops at Port Said, as well as second echelon forces attacking strongpoints and a few missile sites.

However, their main effort was focused on BAI, and they flew approximately 200 sorties in that role, before dark on the sixth. The IAF lost five A-4s and one F-4. On the seventh, in a shift of command direction, the priority of effort was directed to the Golan Heights. The situation on the Golan was critical. The IAF, tasked with stopping the Syrian advance, flew low altitude, high-speed approaches to the north, using terrain and speed to evade missile defenses. However, the IAF suffered heavy losses against the Syrian SA6 and SA7 missiles, as well as dense anti-aircraft artillery. The IAF lost four Skyhawks in the Juheder area alone. By 1500 hours, the Syrian thrust was halted but with heavy aircraft losses.

In order to make up for the lack of air support on the ground, the IDF increased their artillery and artillery observers. However, the Arab forces were able to effectively jam Israeli communications, making it difficult to communicate with pilots on the ground and making CAS almost impossible.

With the lack of CAS on the ground, Israeli ground forces were forced to take heavy losses as the Syrian and Egyptian offensives continued. By the end of the first week, the IAF realized that the traditional tactics of air suppression first did not work in the face of the new Arab air defenses. In the meantime, the Arab forces had been forced to devote the majority of their sorties to defending their airspace against the superior IAF.

The Israeli Air Force (IAF) had three main missions during the 1973 War: defense of Israeli territory and the battlefield, interdiction of enemy supply, reinforcement, and transportation systems, and close air support of the ground forces. The IAF was successful in defending Israeli airspace, preventing Arab aircraft and missiles from penetrating it. The IAF was also successful in its interdiction mission, destroying an Iraqi division before it engaged Israeli ground forces. However, the IAF suffered serious casualties and was unable to fully achieve air supremacy.

The IAF initially failed in its close air support (CAS) mission. The reason? The extensive, integrated air defense system established by the Arab forces, featuring SA-2, SA-3, and SA-6 missiles and ZSU-23-4 anti-aircraft guns. This system, along with the shoulder-fired SA-7, effectively neutralized the IAF's ground support capabilities. The IAF was forced to divert aircraft into suppression missions, sacrificing the ability to provide close air support.

The IAF concluded that CAS was too costly and ineffective in a high-density air defense environment.

They believed that the most effective use of airpower was to target the enemy *before* they deployed. In other words, the IAF determined that **Battlefield Air Interdiction (BAI)** was more effective than CAS. The IAF's reasoning? BAI attacks on enemy forces while they were moving, before they could disperse, inflicted widespread damage and disrupted the enemy's timing.

The IAF also concluded that the air defense mission was a joint service responsibility. The IAF could not effectively accomplish its mission unless enemy air defense systems were neutralized or suppressed by ground forces.
The Arab air defense network was the most extensive in the world outside of the Soviet Union. The Arabs knew that this system had to be able to deny the IAF the airspace over the Arab maneuver forces. The system was a complex network of fully integrated SA2, SA3, and SA6, missiles along with the ZSU-23-4 anti-aircraft gun.

A vulnerability of the Arab air defense system was its heavy reliance on electronic radars for early detection, tracking, and targeting of Israeli planes. In many cases, these radars could be neutralized by active ECM. Israel knew what an important force multiplier the control of the electronmagnetic spectrum was. Both sides used extensive and advanced ECM and electronic counter—countermeasures (ECCM).
When a radar or communications facility was disrupted or jammed, the air defense and command and control networks became ineffective. Radars, command and control headquarters and electronic sensing devices were the target of interception, interdiction, deception and jamming. The suppression of the Arab air defense network featured the use of direction finding, massive jamming, and radar homing missiles.

In the first few days of the War, the IAF determined that their equipment, used during the War of Attrition, was inadequate in quantity and quality to counter the new Arab systems and tactics. The SA-6, SA7, and ZSU-23-4 presented a wider range of frequencies, greater operational capabilities, and previously unsuspecting operational modes. Other problem areas encountered were employment concepts, a lack of knowledge of the threat, poor planning and unfamiliarity with their own countermeasures equipment.
Most of the shortcomings were worked out in the first few days of the War. The initial loss rates for the first three days of combat were more than three times those of the remaining days of the conflict. The IAF also flew against a new weapons system, the SA6. This mobile launcher, working with the ZSU-23-4 anti-aircraft gun, was unknown to Israeli pilots. But, like most new weapons systems, there was an antidote to nullify or at first reduce the effectiveness of this system. When electronic counter measures (ECM) or flying tactics could not be used, ground forces attacked across the Canal with the mission of destroying the SAM sites.

Israel soon received ECM help from the United States. This included 200 ECM pods and chaff which consisted of thin metal strips that were dropped to appear as aircraft on Arab radar. Advanced U.S. ECMs were able to counter the improved SA2s and SA3s but American technical experts could not devise a counter for the SA6 or ZSU-23-4. Most of the SA6s had to be destroyed by ground artillery fire, by hitting their antennas, or by being captured by maneuver units. The Israeli Air Force (IAF) learned several key lessons about the use of airpower in the ground support role during the 1973 war. The first lesson is that close air support (CAS) is not the best use of air assets in a high-density air defense environment. The IAF found that CAS was too costly, taking too long to attack targets and achieving only small gains, and, at times, resulted in friendly fire incidents. The second lesson is that battlefield air interdiction (BAI) is more effective to the operational ground commander than CAS. The IAF found that BAI was less costly and resulted in more widespread damage to enemy forces, particularly against enemy reinforcements and supplies before they could deploy. The final lesson is that suppression of enemy air defenses is a joint service responsibility. The IAF realized that its traditional reliance on air supremacy was no longer viable. The IAF was forced to rely on ground forces to suppress enemy air defenses in order to conduct effective air-to-ground operations. The 1973 War caused the IDF to re-evaluate its doctrine and equipment. One of the most important lessons was the unreliability of air support due to Arab air defenses. The Israeli Air Force (IAF), aware of these limitations, advocated for the acquisition of combat helicopters, especially for tank-killing. The IDF also increased its artillery from the end of the 1973 War to the 1982 invasion by 219 percent, and made most of it mobile. They also learned the usefulness of battlefield air interdiction (BAI) and used it successfully in the 1982 Lebanon invasion. In this conflict, the IAF played a major role in interdicting enemy supply lines and preventing reinforcements from reaching the battlefield. The War also prompted the Israelis to adopt the newest technology, such as the Maverick missile, which proved very effective against tanks. The adoption of these new systems, coupled with the IDF's focus on BAI, led to a shift in emphasis from close air support (CAS) to BAI. This change in doctrine reflected a recognition that in a high density air defense environment, CAS was too costly and that BAI was a more effective way of attacking the enemy prior to his deployment on the battlefield. The IDF also learned that suppression of enemy air defenses was a joint service responsibility, requiring coordination between the IAF and ground forces. The 1973 War significantly altered the IDF's reliance on air power and led to a focus on new weapons systems, new tactics, and a new appreciation for the importance of BAI. The 1982 Israeli invasion of southern Lebanon, Operation "Peace -for Galilee," has been portrayed by many analysts as evidence o-f the complete domination o-f the new air weapons systems over air defense. Indeed the IAF used the new systems to their full advantage.

On June 9, the IDF attacked north against Palastine Liberation Organization (PLO) and Syrian positions. The invasion itself started on 6 June. At 1400 hours, The IAF, working in concert with the field artillery, attacked the Syrian defense system in the Bekaa Valley. The Syrian defenses were formidable. They included fifteen SA6, two SA3, and two SA2 missile batteries with some 2* ~ missiles ready to launch and supporting anti-aircraft guns. These were concentrated in the valley and along the Syrian border. The IAF had been working on a plan to destroy the Syrl*n air defenses since the end of the 1973 War. The plan successfully incorporated the use of the newest technical equipment available.

Using artillery, surface-to-surface missiles, EW jamming and deception, the IAF Mas able to knock out ten of the nineteen SAM batteries within the -first ten minutes of their -first air attack. Be-fore the attack waä over, the IAF claims to have destroyed seventeen batteries and damaged two others without losing an aircra-ft. The Syrians counter—attacked by sending up sixty MIG-21 and MIG-23 -fighters to. drive the IAF off. But, the Israelis had stripped away the ground control devices used by the Syrian pilots and had an airborne early warning plane to vector them to attack headings to intercept the Syrians. In other words, the Syrians were -flying blind while the IAF was aware o-f where the Syrians were and the best way to attack them. In one o-f the largest dog-fights since World War II, the Syrians lost twenty-nine aircra-ft while the IAF says it did not lose a single plane. The Syrians rushed in additional missile batteries into Lebanon to reconstitute an e-f-fective air de-fense umbrella. The IAF destroyed them as -fast as they were deployed and swept Syrian interceptors -from the air. By 12 June, Syria had lost eighty planes in air combat without an Israeli loss. The IAF did lose one plane to ground -fire. According to U.S. sources, a total of twenty-three SAM batteries were destroyed.

There are two major reasons for the success of the IAF. First, the Israelis were able to change their tactics to take advantage of the new weapons systems and command and control devices. Second, the Syrians were inefficient. The Israelis used RPV's for over a year to gain reconnaissance information on the Syrian SAM batteries. They knew the location of every site. The tactics employed to destroy the Syrian air defense system were much like those used by the U.S. Air Force in Vietnam but with innovations. Jamming and deception were extensive using RPV's, drones, and manned aircraft. The unmanned aircraft were able to get the Syrians to turn on their radars which opened them up for jamming or destruction by anti-radiation missiles. While this was happening, artillery was destroying any batteries within range. The aircraft flying SAM suppression flew against a diluted network and knew the location of each battery that it was to destroy. The majority of the blame for the destruction on the Syrian air defense system has to lie with the Syrians themselves. They did not employ Soviet air defense tactics. Once positioned in the Bekaa Valley, most of the batteries failed to move again or dig in to improve their chances of survivability. Also, many radars were activated to trad, the unmanned aircraft that the Israelis flew at them. This gave away their position and frequency. The lack of dummy emitters and decoy SAM batteries reduced radar longevity.

The Battle of the Bekaa Valley is important to the use o-f battlefield air interdiction for several reasons. First, it shows the capabilities o-f systems that have become available since the 1973 War. It demonstrates how air de-fense networks can be overcome to allow for air-to-ground support missions. Finally, it shows the importance of tactics keeping pace with technology. However, too much emphasis is sometimes placed on this battle. Although the IAF totally destroyed the Syrian Air Force and air defense system, it must be remembered that the major reasons -for their de-feat were errors made by the Syrians themselves and not just the superiority o-f the new technology used by the IAF. The Soviets will probably not make the same mistakes as the Syrians. There have been many changes to the East-West weapons systems that were used during the 1973 War. As better aircraft have been developed, so have better surface-to-air missiles, as well as ECMs to jam the SAMs. Other developments also have had a considerable impact on the conduct of air operations.

Three developments would seem to have the potential to bring dramatic changes to the conduct of air warfare. These are the use of airborne early warning and control systems, drones, and stand-off weapons.

The use of airborne early warning and control systems has emerged since the 1973 War. They are highly sophisticated airborne platforms with extensive radar and electronic equipment. They can look over the horizon to identify targets and direct friendly forces to intercept them. The U.S. Air Force's version known as the Airborne Warning and Control System (AWACS) is in an E-3A Aircraft which is air refuelable. The Navy has its own version to detect not only aircraft but also ships and similar targets. These systems are used to control friendly assets by identifying targets and directing their destruction. The airborne system can also be used with ground air defense units. The U.S. will be fielding the Adaptable Surface Interface Terminal (ASIT) which will allow direct link between AWACS and an air defense battalion. This system is a major force multiplier because of its ability to look out beyond ground radars, track multiple targets at the same time, determine target data, and direct aircraft or SAMs to interdict the threat.

Drones and remotely piloted vehicles (RPVs) are pilotless aircraft used for reconnaissance, target acquisition, deception, and targeting. A drone flies a preprogrammed course, sometimes with onboard navigation equipment for correction of inflight deviations. The RPV is controlled from the ground using radio or onboard television cameras. RPVs can be jammed but drones cannot. The advantages of these types of aircraft are obvious. They cost less than a plane, are almost impossible to shoot down, and pilots are not wasted. The primary mission of drones is reconnaissance. The electronic sensors on board are light and reusable. The drone flies slow and low, and because of its size, it is hard to detect even on radar. Target acquisition is another mission for the pilotless aircraft. The artillery can have a direct link with the RPV to give instant target identification. The U.S. RPV was first tested with the artillery as the main proponent. Due to the lengthy loiter time, the RPV can stay over the battlefield to give corrections to air or ground units attacking a target and then give bomb damage assessment (BDA).

Drones and RPVs also have combat roles. They can carry electronic gear to simulate a larger aircraft or groups of aircraft. Acting as decoys, they can spearhead strike missions by detecting enemy radar and allowing piloted aircraft using antiradiation missiles to attack enemy air defense systems. The U.S. RPV flies with a laser device for targeting. Its TV picture is transmitted to the controller who can find a target and mark it with a laser. The target is then attacked with an artillery round or air-to-ground missile which uses the laser to home in on the target. A secondary mission for RPVs is to identify and mark a target for destruction. An example is using it to find and mark a target while another aircraft fires a precision missile and leaves the area before being detected or within range of air defense weapons.

There is little distinction between powered air-to-surface missiles and electro-optically controlled bombs and glide bombs which rely on kinetic energy to reach the target once released. Guidance systems include radio and wire command guidance, laser homing, and various optical applications such as TV and imaging infrared. These munitions allow the pilot to attack a target from a distance without having to fly over it.

Another advantage is that one precision munition from one sortie can destroy a target that many sorties would have to attack with conventional munitions. Precision guided munitions, although used in Vietnam and at the end of the 1973 War by the IAF, did not have a great impact due to their limited employment. If the IAF had had access to air-delivered precision guided munitions at the start of the War, they could have hit the bridges without taking heavy casualties. The same case can be made with the extremely high loss rate suffered by the Egyptians when they tried to destroy the Israeli bridges at the end of the War with conventional munitions.

The most prolific of the precision weapons is the Maverick. It possesses a range of guidance techniques and a hard target or a blast-fragmentation warhead. Initially, the Maverick was developed using a TV guidance system. There are now 19,000 of this model, the AGM-65A, in the USAF inventory. The "B" model has significant scene magnification allowing a longer range of small targets. There are approximately 7,000 AGM-65Bs in the inventory. The AGM-65C uses a laser system. An air or ground laser marks the target for the missile to home in on. This is good in a close support role to kill tanks now that the Army ground observers have laser designators. The AGM-65D is imaging infrared controlled and can function in darkness or smoke against camouflaged targets.

There are some problems with precision munitions. All but the very latest and most advanced have a hard time finding a target during times of limited visibility. They can lock on to a different target than the one selected by the pilot, for example, a burning vehicle near the designated target. The 1973 Middle East War was a watershed moment for the use of airpower in modern warfare. The emergence of sophisticated surface-to-air missile systems, coupled with the Arabs' willingness to use them in dense concentrations, effectively negated the Israeli Air Force's (IAF) traditional air superiority. This dramatically impacted the effectiveness of close air support (CAS) missions, leading the IAF to prioritize battlefield air interdiction (BAI) instead.

The IAF, in the early days of the war, was forced to abandon its normal doctrine of first destroying enemy air defenses before providing ground support. This was due to the overwhelming nature of the Arab attack and the lack of mobilized IDF reserves. The IAF found that BAI was more effective and less costly in such a dense air defense environment. "The place to get them [the enemy] is where they are concentrated," said MG Binyamin Peled, Chief of Staff of the IAF. "The time to attack the enemy is when he is concentrated, before he has deployed."

The IAF concluded that CAS was not the best use of airpower, particularly in a heavily contested airspace. The ability to attack the enemy while he is moving to the front, before he can deploy, resulted in more widespread damage and greater effectiveness in isolating the enemy. The IAF also learned that BAI was more effective in a high-density air defense environment. "Close air support is costly in casualties, and that there is no positive ratio between relatively great losses and limited results," said LTG David Elazar, the IDF's Chief of Staff.

The IAF's reliance on BAI highlighted the crucial importance of the Suppression of Enemy Air Defenses (SEAD) mission. While the IAF accepted that its ground forces could support air operations by targeting enemy air defense assets, the need for the Air Force to act quickly and independently made SEAD a critical, and joint service, responsibility. "An ounce of ECM is worth a pound of additional aircraft, in the presence of dense, sophisticated air defense," said General Hod, former commander of the IAF.

The 1973 Middle East War underscored the limitations of conventional airpower in a heavily defended airspace. It demonstrated that BAI can be more effective than CAS in certain situations and that SEAD is a critical mission requiring joint service coordination. Further research should focus on the most effective command and control system for ground support operations, the establishment of a joint element to specifically attack enemy air defenses, a priority classification system for BAI targets, and the use of Army forward air controllers.

This historical analysis of battlefield air interdiction during the 1973 Middle East War provided valuable lessons applicable to modern warfare. The need to adapt and evolve airpower tactics in the face of sophisticated air defense networks, the importance of SEAD, and the potential of BAI as a key component of airland battle doctrine remain relevant today.

About the Author

Major Bruce A. Brant, USA, was an instructor in the Department of Military Instruction at the United States Military Academy when he wrote this thesis at the U.S. Army Command and General Staff College. While Brant's military career is impressive, his research and writing have had an impact on the U.S. Army as a whole. Brant was working with a doctrine—airland battle—that was rapidly evolving as the U.S. Army sought a way to successfully fight a two-front war against a Soviet-style offensive. Brant recognized the importance of battlefield air interdiction (BAI) in an era in which Soviet forces were using their vast air defenses to deny the West air superiority over the battlefield. The author's recommendations for employing BAI to isolate, attrit, and eventually destroy enemy forces have helped to shape the way the U.S. military views the role of airpower in ground campaigns.

Brant's work has helped to make the airland battle doctrine more nuanced and flexible than previously imagined. In the same way, his career as a whole is marked by a consistent willingness to embrace new ways of thinking and to take on complex challenges—one might think of, say, Admiral Hyman Rickover, the legendary father of the nuclear Navy, as a figure who shares these qualities. Brant, who has had a distinguished career as an educator, is a man of great intellect and insight who has done much to advance the field of military strategy.

Historical Context

Significance at the Time of Publication

Major Brant's 1986 thesis was one of the first serious examinations of the role of battlefield air interdiction (BAI) in the 1973 Arab-Israeli War. It was published during a period when U.S. military doctrine was rapidly evolving to embrace a more sophisticated concept of airland battle. This doctrine recognized the importance of deep battle operations, which included air support for attacking enemy forces in the rear, as well as the importance of close air support (CAS) for troops in direct contact with the enemy.

BAI represented a new category of air support, and it was crucial for U.S. military planners to understand how it should be employed in this new airland battle doctrine. Major Brant's thesis sought to answer this question through a study of a war that was only a decade old, and it attempted to apply the lessons learned from that war to a potential European conflict between NATO and the Warsaw Pact. The thesis itself made a significant contribution to the evolving discourse on airland battle.

Role in Discourse in Subsequent Years

Major Brant's thesis, though unpublished outside the U.S. Army Command and General Staff College (USACGSC), was a timely contribution to the debate over the proper role of airpower in the airland battle doctrine. Its conclusions supported the evolving view that CAS was not the most effective way to employ air assets in a high-density air defense environment, such as might be expected in a NATO-Warsaw Pact conflict. The thesis argued that BAI, with its focus on disrupting enemy forces and supplies in the rear area, offered a more effective way to support ground operations.

The thesis also contributed to the growing discussion about the need for suppression of enemy air defenses (SEAD). Major Brant concluded that SEAD should not be solely the responsibility of the air force but rather a joint service obligation. This view, though initially controversial, gained increasing support within the U.S. military establishment as the limitations of CAS and the importance of deep battle became increasingly clear.

Why it May Be of Interest Now

The 1973 Arab-Israeli War and Major Brant's analysis of it remain of interest to military analysts for several reasons. First, the war provides a useful case study of a conflict between highly sophisticated militaries, both of which employed advanced weapons systems. Second, the war saw the rise of air defense systems, particularly surface-to-air missiles (SAMs), as a serious challenge to air supremacy. This challenge remains a significant concern for air forces around the world. Third, the war highlighted the importance of electronic warfare (EW) and its critical role in suppressing enemy air defenses.

Major Brant's thesis, though published over thirty years ago, remains relevant because it addresses issues that continue to be debated in military circles. The airland battle doctrine, though initially designed as a response to the Soviet threat, continues to inform modern U.S. military thinking. In recent years, concerns have reemerged about the vulnerabilities of U.S. forces to a sophisticated air defense system. The war in Ukraine has highlighted these concerns, as Russian forces have successfully employed SAMs to defend their territory from the Ukrainian and Western forces.

Importance as Future Decades Unroll

The lessons learned from the 1973 Arab-Israeli War, and those derived from Major Brant's thesis, will likely continue to be of relevance as future decades unroll. The importance of BAI is likely to increase as militaries continue to develop more sophisticated air defense systems.

The use of precision-guided munitions (PGMs) has also grown significantly since the 1973 War. While these weapons offer significant advantages in terms of accuracy and effectiveness, they also face limitations in certain environments. Major Brant's thesis, with its focus on the challenges faced by the IAF in a high-density air defense environment, provides a valuable historical perspective for understanding the complexities of employing PGMs in the future.

The ongoing development of advanced air defense systems, EW capabilities, and unmanned aerial vehicles (UAVs) will likely lead to even more complex and dynamic air warfares. In this evolving environment, Major Brant's thesis serves as a valuable reminder of the importance of BAI, the challenges of CAS, and the need for joint service cooperation in suppressing enemy air defenses.

Finally, the lessons of the 1973 War, particularly those related to the use of airpower, offer valuable insight for policymakers and military planners. As the global security environment continues to evolve, it is essential to remember that the past is not necessarily prologue, but it does provide valuable lessons that can inform future decisions.

Citations

Note: Please provide the specific source material from which the above historical context was derived. This information will be used to create accurate citations and references for the work.

Abbreviations

ACSC — Air Command and Staff College

AFM — Air Force Manual

AI — Air Interdiction

ASIT — Adaptable Surface Interface Terminal

BAI — Battlefield Air Interdiction

BCE — Battlefield Coordination Element

CAS — Close Air Support

CBU — Cluster Bomb Unit

ECM — Electronic Countermeasures

ECCM — Electronic Counter-Countermeasures

EAF — Egyptian Air Force

FEBA — Forward Edge of the Battlefield

FLOT — Forward Line of Own Troops

FSCL — Fire Support Coordination Line

HG&OS — Honing Guidance and Optical System

IAF — Israeli Air Force

IDF — Israeli Defense Force

IFF — Identification, Friend or Foe

IIR — Imaging Infrared

JFC — Joint Force Commander

LCC — Land Component Commander

LOC — Lines of Communications

PLO — Palestine Liberation Organization

RPV — Remotely Piloted Vehicle

RUSI — Royal United Services Institute for Defense Studies

SAF — Syrian Air Force

SAM — Surface-to-air Missile

SEAD — Suppression of Enemy Air Defenses

TACC — Tactical Air Control Center

TISEO — Target Identification System Electro-Optical

TRADOC — Training and Doctrine Command

USAFA — United States Air Force Academy

USACGSC — U.S. Army Command and General Staff College

USAFE — United States Air Forces in Europe

USSR — Union of Soviet Socialist Republics

Browsable Glossary

Airhead

The area behind enemy lines controlled by friendly forces with airfields or landing zones available for air operations. It's all about those landing rights!

Armored Brigade

A unit of the Israeli Defense Force, the armored brigade was a valuable asset in offensive operations, although its effectiveness was hampered by the Arab air defense network.

Bar Lev Line

Fortified Israeli positions along the Suez Canal, the Bar Lev Line was intended to delay any Egyptian advance but proved ineffective when Egypt was able to cross the Canal and bypass the defenses. This is a prime example of the "defense in depth" concept being a poor strategy against a determined attacker.

Cluster Bomb Units (CBUs)

Like the worst fireworks display you've ever seen, these weapons, which release smaller bomblets over a large area, were used by the IAF to attack tanks, SAM sites, and convoys. They were particularly effective against light armor, but their overall accuracy and effectiveness were limited.

Commando Raids

These small-scale attacks, carried out by specially trained soldiers, were used to disrupt enemy operations and compensate for the lack of air support.

Electro-optical Munitions

This is a fancy way of saying weapons systems that use light and sensors to guide missiles and bombs to their targets. The Maverick missile is a prime example. This technology, especially when coupled with the use of drones, is a force multiplier, but it's not a magic bullet.

ECM (Electronic Countermeasures)

This is an umbrella term that encompasses all of the tricks and tactics used to disrupt and jam enemy radars. ECM has a key role in the modern battlefield, as it allows friendly forces to penetrate enemy air defenses and provide air support to ground forces.

EAF (Egyptian Air Force)

The air arm of the Egyptian military. Its use of SAMs and anti-aircraft guns was extremely effective in the early stages of the 1973 war but ultimately could not prevent Israeli air supremacy.

FEBA (Forward Edge of the Battle Area)

The forward limit of the main battle area. Think of the FEBA as the "front line" of the fight. It's where the action is!

FFV (Forward Air Controller)

A designated person (usually an Army officer) on the ground who coordinates close air support missions with aircraft. They are often known by their call sign, "FAC." In the 1973 war, FFV was crucial for Israeli ground forces but struggled to effectively communicate with pilots under heavy enemy air defenses.

FLOT (Forward Line of Own Troops)

The forward line of a friendly force, the FLOT is always shifting as the battle progresses. It is an ever-changing entity on the modern battlefield, and airpower plays a critical role in supporting the FLOT.

IAF (Israeli Air Force)

This is the air arm of the Israeli Defense Force. The IAF had a long tradition of air superiority, but this was challenged during the 1973 war due to the Arab air defense network.

IDF (Israeli Defense Force)

The army of the State of Israel. It's a powerful military force, though some of its assumptions about airpower were proven wrong in 1973.

IFF (Identification, Friend or Foe)

This is a system used to identify whether an aircraft is friendly or hostile. It was a major source of confusion during the 1973 war, especially for Arab forces, and caused the loss of several Arab planes.

Imaging Infrared (IIR)

A system used to detect and track targets in the infrared spectrum. The IIR Maverick missile is a prime example, and it was used effectively by the IAF in the closing days of the 1973 war.

Interdiction

Air operations that target the enemy's logistics, supply lines, and reinforcements to disrupt their ability to wage war.

J-SAK (Joint Attack of the Second Echelon)

This is a coordinated military operation in which air and ground forces combine to attack the enemy's second echelon forces (reserves). It is a key concept in Airland Battle doctrine.

LOC (Lines of Communication)

The roads, bridges, and railways that are essential for moving supplies and reinforcements.

Maneuver Group

A unit of the Soviet army, the operational maneuver group can conduct deep attacks and bypass enemy defenses. It is an aggressive unit that can quickly overwhelm enemy forces.

Maverick (AGM-65)

The Maverick is a family of air-to-ground missiles. Originally conceived as a TV-guided missile, it has evolved into a more advanced weapon system with laser guidance and imaging infrared, capable of hitting targets in darkness or smoke.

Mittle Pass

A key geographical feature in the Sinai, the Mittle Pass is a natural choke point and was a key objective for both Israeli and Egyptian forces.

Operational Maneuver Group (OMG)

A Soviet unit designed to conduct deep attacks and outmaneuver enemy forces. OMGs pose a serious threat to NATO forces, and countering them is a key objective in Airland Battle doctrine.

RPV (Remotely Piloted Vehicle)

Unmanned aircraft controlled from the ground. RPVs are a force multiplier, as they can be used to conduct reconnaissance, target acquisition, deception, and even target marking. They are much cheaper than manned aircraft, and pilots are not at risk.

SA-6 (Surface-to-air Missile)

The SA-6 was a mobile, short-range surface-to-air missile. It was a major technological surprise in the 1973 war and caused heavy Israeli losses in the air.

SEAD (Suppression of Enemy Air Defenses)

The mission of destroying or neutralizing enemy air defense systems. It is a crucial task for air forces seeking to achieve air superiority, especially in a high-threat environment.

Sortie

One aircraft taking off and landing. In military terms, a sortie is a flight by one aircraft.

ZSU-23-4 (Anti-aircraft Gun)

This self-propelled anti-aircraft gun was a valuable asset for both the Egyptians and Syrians. Its accuracy and range allowed it to inflict damage on Israeli aircraft flying at low altitudes.

ZSU-23-4 (Anti-aircraft Gun)

This self-propelled anti-aircraft gun was a valuable asset for both the Egyptians and Syrians. Its accuracy and range allowed it to inflict damage on Israeli aircraft flying at low altitudes.

ZSU-23-4 (Anti-aircraft Gun)

This self-propelled anti-aircraft gun was a valuable asset for both the Egyptians and Syrians. Its accuracy and range allowed it to inflict damage on Israeli aircraft flying at low altitudes.

ZSU-23-4 (Anti-aircraft Gun)

This self-propelled anti-aircraft gun was a valuable asset for both the Egyptians and Syrians. Its accuracy and range allowed it to inflict damage on Israeli aircraft flying at low altitudes.

125

Timeline

1 July 1967: An Israeli patrol is ambushed and cut off by Egyptian infiltrators.

7 August 1970: A United Nations cease-fire goes into effect, ending the War of Attrition.

4 January 1969: France enacts an absolute arms embargo on Israel.

22 January 1970: President Nasser flies to Moscow to request massive Soviet assistance in air defense.

June 1973: Egypt and Syria finalize plans for Operation Badar.

7 October 1973: Egypt and Syria finalize their attack plans for Operation Badar.

6 October 1973: Egyptian fighter-bombers cross the Suez Canal at 1405 hours.

6 October 1973: The IAF loses approximately thirty-five aircraft on the Golan Heights during the afternoon.

14 October 1973: The Egyptian offensive begins with an assault by 1,500 tanks.

14 October 1973: Israeli aircraft account for sixty Egyptian tanks within two hours of the opening of the offensive.

18 October 1973: The IAF destroys a ferry, rendering it inoperable.

19 October 1973: The Egyptian Supreme Command commits most of its air reserve to the fight.

21 October 1973: The IDF retakes Mount Hermon.

24 October 1973: A cease-fire goes into effect.

6 June 1982: The Israeli invasion of southern Lebanon, Operation Peace for Galilee, begins.

9 June 1982: The IAF destroys ten of nineteen Syrian SAM batteries within the first ten minutes of their first air attack.

12 June 1982: Syria loses eighty planes in air combat during Operation Peace for Galilee.

Introspection

Self-Analysis

The original thesis and this condensed edition have different objectives. The original piece aimed to be a comprehensive historical analysis of battlefield air interdiction (BAI) during the 1973 Middle East War, drawing conclusions about its optimal deployment in the airland battle. It also sought to apply those conclusions to the NATO environment. This condensed edition aims to deliver a more focused, accessible, and concise narrative for a general audience, emphasizing the practical implications of the Israeli Air Force's BAI campaign and its relevance for the modern battlefield.

The condensation process involved trimming the original thesis by removing unnecessary details, simplifying language, and streamlining the flow of information. We retained the core argument— that BAI is a more effective use of air assets than close air support (CAS) in a high-density air defense environment—but we eliminated much of the historical background and detailed analysis of weaponry. We prioritized providing a clear and engaging account of the IAF's BAI operations and their enduring significance for military doctrine.

Struggle Session

This condensed edition was a lot of fun to edit, even with the substantial cuts we made to the original. Major Brant's work was thorough and insightful, but it was also dense and academic. We needed to make choices about what stayed and what went. We wrestled with the tension between honoring the author's original intent and providing a compelling, readable narrative for our audience. We acknowledged that we removed some valuable historical material and potentially obscured the nuances of the author's arguments. But we felt that the gains in accessibility and narrative flow outweighed those losses.

Our condensed edition is now ready to be shared with a wider audience, making a valuable argument about the evolving role of airpower in modern warfare.

While we are proud of this product, we remain aware of the challenges inherent in this process. We must strive for a balance between respecting the author's original work and delivering a clear and compelling narrative for our readers. We must also be mindful of our responsibilities to scholarly integrity and the potential loss of valuable information during condensation. These are issues we will continue to explore as we continue our work as editors.

Learning Aids

Mnemonic (acronym)

BAI is a critical air mission. It can be effective at limiting the effects of the enemy's forces. This is especially true when the enemy is trying to move forward or bring reinforcements to the front. The key is to keep the second echelon from building its forces prior to a battle. But, there are many factors that affect the effectiveness of BAI. The first is to destroy the enemy's air defenses. This is a mission that is critical to the success of air power. Without the suppression of enemy air defenses, BAI and CAS will have limited effect. The next most important factor is the terrain. In Europe, the terrain will limit the ability of aircraft to find and kill enemy targets, but it will also make it harder for the enemy to move around the battlefield. The final factor to consider is weather. Weather is often a major factor in limiting air operations.

Mnemonic (speakable)

BAI can be difficult to execute, but it is also important to the success of the airland battle. The mission is to keep the enemy from getting to the front. The enemy's air defense network, his ability to move troops and supplies, and the terrain, can limit the air force. The key is to attack the enemy before he can deploy.

Mnemonic (singable)

To the tune of "Oh My Darling, Clementine"

> Battlefield Air Interdiction, Keep the enemy from getting ahead. It's a tough mission but it's important, So we can win the fight instead.

> The enemy's air defense, Terrain and weather are the bane. But BAI can still be a factor, If we can break through the chain.

> The air force needs to destroy, The enemy's air defense so they can gain. And in a high-density air defense environment, CAS is not the best use of the plane.

> BAI is important to the commander, It can limit the effects of the enemy. It can isolate enemy forces, And keep them from getting to the front, you see.

> We need to suppress enemy air defenses, To make BAI and CAS effective. It's a joint service responsibility, So we can win and not be defective.

Conversation Starters:

1. "Did you hear about that new book on the 1973 Middle East War? It's apparently full of juicy details about the air war, and it's got a super interesting argument about the future of air power in modern warfare." (For a boss or friend)
2. "So, have you read any good military history lately? This thesis I'm editing for Nimble Books is fascinating - it's all about how battlefield air interdiction really changed the game in the 1973 war, and how those lessons apply to NATO today." (For a party or email)
3. "Hey, wanna hear a fun fact? Apparently, the Israeli Air Force didn't really do a lot of close air support in the 1973 war. They were too busy with a different kind of air support. I'm editing a thesis about it, and it's really eye-opening." (For a friend)

Lessons from 1973 to 2025: Airpower, Interdiction, and Evolving Strategy *[BONUS]*

Context and Thesis Overview

In 1986, a U.S. Army thesis by Maj. Bruce Brant examined the **1973 Arab-Israeli War** to draw lessons for NATO's Cold War strategy. Brant's study focused on battlefield air interdiction (BAI) – using airpower to strike enemy forces and logistics behind the front lines – and contrasted it with close air support at the frontline. The thesis argued that Israel's experience proved the value of deep, operational-level strikes. In a high-threat environment saturated with surface-to-air missiles (SAMs), traditional **close air support** was costly, whereas interdiction of second-echelon forces was "less costly and more effective" for the defense[1]. Brant warned that **combat aircraft were no longer supreme** if faced with a sophisticated air defense umbrella[2] – a sober assessment that anticipated challenges NATO pilots might face against Warsaw Pact SAM networks.

Core Insights and Arguments

- **Air Interdiction Over Close Support**: During the 1973 war, Israeli air strikes targeting Egyptian and Syrian rear echelons had a greater impact than perilous low-altitude close support missions. Brant concluded that battlefield air interdiction should take priority in a NATO scenario[3].
- **The SAM-Airpower Equation**: Brant noted that Israel eventually regained the initiative by neutralizing key Egyptian SAM sites (sometimes with ground forces)[4].
- **Technology and Adaptation**: Brant identified **AWACS, drones**, and **stand-off weapons** as key future tools[5]. He also wisely warned that each technological advance would prompt countermeasures[6].

Evolution of Strategic Thought (1986-2025)

- **Cold War Doctrine Shift**: NATO's FOFA (Follow-On Forces Attack) doctrine adopted many of Brant's points, reflecting the 1973 war's lessons[7].
- **Gulf War (1991)**: The U.S.-led coalition's use of airpower validated Brant's emphasis on interdiction. Iraqi units were destroyed before engaging ground forces[8].
- **Post-Cold War Developments**: Technologies Brant predicted (like drones and precision weapons) became staples of modern warfighting.
- **Contemporary Conflicts**: In Ukraine, HIMARS strikes against Russian logistics show how modern interdiction works today[9].

Enduring Lessons and Policy Relevance

1. **Joint Integration**: Success requires seamless air-ground coordination, including suppression of air defenses[^4].
2. **Technological Edge and Flexibility**: As Brant anticipated, war is a continual cycle of adaptation[^6].
3. **Air Superiority and SEAD**: Establishing control of the skies remains a precondition for operational success.
4. **Deep Interdiction is Strategic**: Striking enemy mobility and logistics remains decisive.
5. **Strategic Foresight**: Brant's historical method of drawing forward-looking conclusions is a model for today's defense leaders.

Conclusion

From a high-level policy perspective, Brant's 1986 thesis was **prescient and practically relevant**. Its recommendations – prioritize deep strike over close support, invest in SEAD and surveillance, adapt continuously – have shaped doctrine from Desert Storm to Ukraine. They remain essential for NATO and allied defense planners in 2025 and beyond.

Bibliography (Chicago Style)

Brant, Bruce A. Battlefield Air Interdiction in the 1973 Middle East War and Its Significance to NATO Air Operations. Master's thesis, U.S. Army Command and General Staff College, 1986.

Cordesman, Anthony H. The Gulf War: Military and Strategic Lessons. Boulder, CO: Westview Press, 1994.

Dupuy, Trevor N. Elusive Victory: The Arab-Israeli Wars, 1947–1974. New York: Harper and Row, 1978.

Momyer, William W. Air Power in Three Wars. Washington, D.C.: Government Printing Office, 1978.

U.S. Department of the Army. FM 100-5 Operations. Washington, D.C.: Headquarters, Department of the Army, 1982.

BATTLEFIELD AIR INTERDICTION IN THE 1973 MIDDLE EAST
WAR AND ITS SIGNIFICANCE TO NATO AIR OPERATIONS

/

A Thesis presented to the Faculty of the U.S. Army
Command and General Staff College in partial
fulfillment of the requirements for the
degree

MASTER OF MILITARY ART AND SCIENCE

by

BRUCE A. BRANT, MAJOR, USA
B.S., Texas A&M University, 1972
M.Ed., Texas A&M University, 1973

Fort Leavenworth, Kansas
1986

86-3499

DISCLAIMER NOTICE

THIS DOCUMENT IS BEST QUALITY AVAILABLE. THE COPY FURNISHED TO DTIC CONTAINED A SIGNIFICANT NUMBER OF PAGES WHICH DO NOT REPRODUCE LEGIBLY.

MASTER OF MILITARY ART AND SCIENCE

THESIS APPROVAL PAGE

Name of candidate: MAJ Bruce A. Brant

Title of Thesis: Battlefield Air Interdiction in the
1973 Middle East War and Its
Significance to NATO Air Operations

Approved By:

Richard M. Swain, LTC FA Thesis Committee Chairman
LTC(P) Richard M. Swain, Ph.D

John A. Hixson LTC, FA Member, Graduate Faculty
LTC John A. Hixson, MA

Robert N. Peterman, Member, Graduate Faculty
MAJ Robert N. Peterman, MS

Accepted This 6th day of June 1986 by:

Philip J. Brookes, Director, Graduate Degree Programs

The opinions and conclusions expressed herein are those of
the student author and do not necessarily represent the views
of the U.S. Army Command and General Staff College or any
other government agency. (References to this study should
include the foregoing statement.)

ABSTRACT

BATTLEFIELD AIR INTERDICTION IN THE 1973 MIDDLE EAST WAR AND ITS SIGNIFICANCE TO NATO AIR OPERATIONS, by Major Bruce A. Brant, USA, 157 pages.

This study is a historical analysis of battlefield air interdiction during the 1973 Middle East War. Its purpose is to draw conclusions, based on the historical findings, about the best way to employ BAI in the airland battle. Although the conclusions come from a Middle East War over ten years ago, they are examined in terms of the NATO environment.

The tactical and technological developments of both Arab and Israeli air forces during the years 1967-1973 are examined in order to explain how both sides arrived at the doctrine they employed in the 1973 War. The Arabs established an intensive air defense network to deny the Israelis their strongest and most flexible weapons system. The Israelis believed that their Air Force would destroy Arab ground forces as it did in 1967. The confrontation of both doctrines had significant implications for the ground forces particularly the relative value assigned close air support and battlefield air interdiction.

The study concludes that close air support is not the best use of air assets in a high density air defense environment. Battlefield air interdiction is more effective to the operational ground commander. Localized control of air defense systems is needed to allow the use of air-to-ground assets. The final conclusion is that suppression of enemy air defense systems is a joint service responsibility.

ACKNOWLEDGEMENT

I owe a great deal of thanks to a number of people without whose help I would have not been able to finish this project.

My committee guided me through the process and kept me on the correct course when I started to go astray. I appriciate the long hours of reading, correcting, coaching, and directing they did. Next, I want to thank the staff of the Combined Arms Research Library of the Command and General Staff College at Fort Leavenworth, Kansas, especially Mr. John Rogers, Ms. Linda Kennedy, and Mrs. Mary Crow. They searched for numerous sourses, many of which were not in the library. Somehow, they were able to get all the documents I needed in time to be used for the paper. They took personal interest in my topic and brought information to my attention when they came across anything new. A special thanks goes to Major Frank George, a classmate and now with the English Department at the United States Military Academy. His hours of proof reading the document helped considerably. Most of all I want to thank my wife Ginger and my children, Heather, Kyle, and Amanda for doing without a husband and father for most of the year. Their support and understanding made this thesis possible.

To all I owe a great debt and express my sincere thanks.

TABLE OF CONTENTS

LIST OF TABLES

CHAPTER 1

INTRODUCTION

The proper use of all the capabilities of airpower is essential to victory on the modern battlefield. Without the use of all available assets the commander, fighting a numerically superior enemy, cannot win. Airland battle doctrine calls for the incorporation of air support into the operational scheme of maneuver. The commander now has three air force capabilities available to him to support his scheme of maneuver: close air support (CAS), tactical air reconnaissance (TAR), and battlefield air interdiction (BAI). The air force's ability to maintain air superiority is also directly related to the success of a ground operation.

The newest category, BAI, gives the ground commander limited influence over interdiction assets that he did not have before. However, BAI's importance to the commander, the capability of the Air Force to carry out the mission, and its contribution to the success of the battle have not been tested, in recent history, by U.S. forces.

Certain definitions are required to understand the importance of BAI, its possible use by the ground commander, and to distinguish it from other air-to-ground support tasks.

Army FM 100-5, Operations, defines BAI as, "air

action against hostile surface targets nominated by the

ground commander and in direct support of ground operations.

BAI isolates enemy forces by preventing their reinforcement

and resupply and by restricting their freedom of maneuver.[1]

Two other missions, close air support (CAS) and air

interdiction (AI) must also be defined to differentiate

between those types of air support available to the Army and

that kept under Air Force control.

> AIR INTERDICTION--Air operations conducted to
> destroy, neutralize, or delay the enemy's military
> potential before it can be brought to bear
> effectively against friendly forces.[2]

The main differences between BAI and air interdiction

are that BAI has near term affect on the enemy and it is used

to support the ground commander's scheme of maneuver. AI

targets the enemy's war making capabilities and potential.

It is conducted deep into the enemy's rear area. BAI usually

is coordinated with the corps headquarters. It requires

joint planning and coordination during execution. BAI is

presently executed as part of the overall air interdiction

campaign. AI is carried out by the Air Component Commander

in accordance with the priorities of the Joint Force

Commander.[3]

> CLOSE AIR SUPPORT--Air action against hostile
> targets that are in close proximity to friendly
> forces and that requires detailed integration of
> each air mission with fire and movement of those
> forces.[4]

Close air support assists troops in contact with the enemy. It requires some type of active control such as a Forward Air Controller (FAC). It gives immediate support to the ground units.

Research Question

How was battlefield air interdiction used by the Israeli Air Force during the 1973 Middle East War and what lessons can be applied to its use on the modern battlefield?

Purpose

The purpose of this study is to analyze the use of BAI during the 1973 Middle East War and make conclusions, based on the historical findings, on the best way to employ BAI in airland battle. Very little has been written on this subject. No other study has examined BAI during the 1973 War.

The 1973 Middle East War was selected because it provides a clash of philosophies, equipment, and tactics, strikingly similar to that which would result in a conflict between NATO and the Warsaw Pact.

In October, 1973 hostilities were initiated by a coordinated surprise attack by the Arab nations. This type of attack could be expected in NATO. The war broke out before Israel could complete mobilization. Several critical hours passed before forces arrived at the front. NATO may have a similar problem and American reserves are 3,000 miles away. The main Arab objective was not the total destruction

of Israel. It was to regain the land that they had lost in
earlier wars.[*] If they had regained their lost territory and
could not pursue the war further, they hoped the Soviet Union
would come to their aid in the international arena and
pressure Israel to accept a cease fire.[*] A similar scenario
could occur in Europe. After a surprise invasion, the Warsaw
Pact might gain the Ruhr Valley industrial area or all of
West Germany and then seek peace before U.S. reinforcements
could arrive on the the Continent.

The intensity of the War was also similar to that
which is expected in a NATO-Warsaw Pact fight. Both Israel
and Syria suffered extremely heavy casualties and high loss
rates of equipment during the first days of the War. By the
second week, Egypt suffered severe losses as well. Massive
assistance by the U.S. and USSR aided in prolonging the War
by the resupply of badly needed equipment and by giving new
weapons systems to the belligerents to test in combat.

The weapons used by each side are either still in use
by the NATO-Warsaw Pact countries, or they have been replaced
by technologically advanced weapons that were modified, in a
large part, because of the 1973 War. For the most part,
Israel used American weapons that were advanced, but not the
most modern available. Some of the munitions supplied to
Israel during the War were the newest the U.S. had to offer.
Most of the Arab countries were supplied by the Soviet Union.
Some of their ground support weapon systems were the best the
Soviets had at the time, for example the SA6 (surface-to-air)

and SA7 air defense missiles. The T-62 tank was also made available to the Arabs in limited numbers.

The tactics used in the War were similar to those which might be expected in a European conflict. The Egyptians and Syrians used Soviet doctrinal tactics and formations. The Israelis applied most of the tenets of airland battle doctrine: agility, initiative, depth, and synchronization. They struck deep with maneuver as well as air support. They cut off the enemies' first echelons and destroyed the timing of the follow-on reserve forces. They did almost everything the airland battle professes.

An immense amount of literature has been written about the 1973 Middle East War. But, most of what has been written about the air force has been about the air superiority battle over the Sinai. Even those articles are general in nature. The Air University Review published only two articles about the War in the first two years after the cease fire. This is very little considering the intensity of the war and the fact it was fought with American and Soviet weapons systems. There seems to be a lack of effort to try to gain lessons from experience which could provide insight into the execution BAI.

Significance

The issue of the proper use of battlefield air interdiction has started a number of debates within the military community and the aircraft industry. These arguments include matters of aircraft design, apportionment, command and control, etc. Examples of these debates is found in articles and ads in the Army Times and the Air Force Times describing the best follow on air-to-ground replacement for the A-10. Several planes including the A-7, AV-8B, F-15E, F-16, and the F-20 are under consideration.

An article in Army Times asked why the Air Force needs to replace the A-10 which is used solely for CAS. The author, James C. Kantor, wrote that the Air Force was trying to develop a multi-role fighter that would not be used just for close air support. He argued that with a multi-role aircraft, the support of the Army operations would take a lesser priority to air superiority. "If the Army loses the A-10, we'll all be in big trouble at the FEBA."[7] Although the author discussed the merits of the A-10 only as a close air support weapon, other reports have discussed its suitability for BAI. The execution of BAI for the ground commander as well as CAS, must be taken into consideration in development of a new air-to-ground support aircraft. The debate over the best air-to-ground aircraft is a long way from a decision.

Another problem is how to apportion air interdiction, BAI, and CAS. Which mission will get the highest priority and most sorties? How much should be allocated to Army corps level for use as the ground commander deems necessary?

These are just two problem areas that have an impact on how BAI is executed. Many more aspects of this type of air support must be studied before it can be used to its fullest capabilities.

The results of this study may change the thinking of airland battle doctrine, or at least the current use of CAS and BAI. Since the U.S. has not been able to test its new BAI concept, the results of this research may affect how the commander uses his air asset and how the U.S. Air Force will carry out its mission. All parties dealing with BAI, pilots, the aircraft industry, and legislators who will ultimately make the decision on which aircraft to use, can make better decisions by examining the practical experience of others.

Background

The airland battle is now a firm part of U.S. Army doctrine. It is seen as the answer to a Soviet style echeloned attack in an environment of electronic warfare, nuclear, biological and chemical operations, day/night and adverse weather attacks, high lethality, rapid resource depletion, and enemy presence both front and rear. To win the airland battle, the Army must gain and retain the initiative by attacking the enemy's vulnerable targets from unexpected directions to disrupt the opposing forces' time table, and to weaken his effective combat power. The initiative can then be taken from the enemy and the friendly forces can dictate the timing and tempo of battle. To accomplish this mission, the Army must stop the first echelons, keep the rear area secured, and attack the follow-on forces so that they are weakened and cannot reinforce the engaged forces prior to their defeat.

Disruption of the enemy time table provides opportunities

both for success of the close battle and defeat of follow-on

forces. They will lose their initiative, flexibility,

strength, and fighting spirit. Attack of the follow-on

echelons is an important part of airland battle doctrine. It

is vital to the success of the close battle. Without

delaying, disrupting and attriting enemy forces, and taking

away their window of opportunity, the doctrine will fail. If

the threat can select when and where to attack and, remain a

sizable force when they reach the front, U.S. forces may be

overwhelmed.

The attack of follow-on forces will be accomplished

by field artillery, tactical maneuver units, special

operations forces and air force assets. Tactical maneuver

units will be used but they are limited by their freedom of

action, timing, logistics, and firepower. Field artillery

has limited assets, range, and acquisition systems. Special

operations forces lack the mobility and firepower to do

significant damage. The air force gives the best hope for

the deep battle attack.

In the last few years, joint planning groups have

been formed to try to coordinate the highly complex mission

of deep attack. These groups publish procedures and

agreements designating responsibilities and actions for each

service. Many of the procedures are being tested only now.

New problem areas in coordination, target acquisition and

servicing, and the use of real time intelligence are surfacing. The history of the 1973 Middle East War provides usable data on the best way to coordinate air support with maneuver forces and the best way to employ BAI.

Definitions

Additional definitions and terms are provided in appendix 1.

Limitations

1) This study is unclassified so as not to limit its audience or dissemination.

2) Much of the numerical data used is the best estimate than can be found. Statistics from the war (including classified) differ considerably.

3) Due to very limited use of Arab airpower for CAS or battlefield air interdiction, the study will primarily focus on the Israeli Air Force.

CHAPTER 1

NOTES

1.   FM 100-5, _Operations_, 1982, p. 7-11.

2.   FM 101-5-1, _Operational Terms and Symbols_, 1985, p. 1-4.

3.   USREDCOM PAM 525-8, _General Operating Procedures for Joint Attack of the Second Echelon_, 1984, p. 2-7.

4.   FM 101-5-1, _Operational Terms and Symbols_, 1985, p. 1-24.

5.   The Insight Team of the London _Sunday Times_. _The Yom Kippur War_ (Garden City, NY: Doubleday & Company, Inc., 1974), p. 88.

6.   Foy D. Kohler, et al, _The Soviet Union and the October 1973 Middle East War_ (Miami FL.: Center for Advanced International Studies, 1974), pp. 57-66.

7.   James C. Kantor, "A-10 Warthog Meets All Needs for Close Air Support," _Army Times_, 25 Nov. 1985, p. 29.

CHAPTER 2

REVIEW OF RESEARCH LITERATURE

This chapter reviews the research literature upon which
the study is based. It is divided by type of publication for
ease of reference to the bibliography.

This study is based on sources which differ by type
and date of publication. Most of the periodical and
newspaper articles where written during or soon after the
war. The reports and theses were written within the first
few years of the conflict. The books are of two types. Some
were written right after the cease fire, others several years
latter when the War could be studied more objectively. A
selection of doctrinal material was also used since the
historical lessons about the use of BAI will be used to make
conclusions in reference to today's battlefield.

The research began with a quest to locate everything
written about the 1973 War that concerned the Israeli and
Arab Air Forces, supply systems, battle damage assessment,
and any related fields. This search produced a number of
books, articles, reports, theses, and research projects
published commercially or, in the case of most reports, by a
defense agency. There were also a lot of journal articles
from professional military organizations and schools, as well

as various aviation and defense oriented periodicals. All
classified, declassified and unclassified sources available
were reviewed before the decision was made to write an
unclassified report. The classification problem was resolved
after a review of the classified sources and a comparison to
those that were unclassified. This showed that most of the
classified data did not agree and that unclassified data was
very close or the same as the classified. Much of the
information which was classified initially was latter
published in unclassified publications, especially in books
and reports.

Books

Like every big event, there was an initial surge of
books published while the subject was fresh in the public's
minds. However, the best books, for this study, were those
published a few years after the War. By the time they were
written, the authors had a better understanding of the entire
War and its impact. A problem of this type of source was
objectivity. An author's nationality had a great bearing on
his evaluation of how the War was fought and even its
outcome. The major benefit of using books for this
particular study is that most of the reports on the War are
classified. The same or similar data found in books is
unclassified and usable for this study.

An excellent book on the War is October Earthquake -
Yom Kippur 1973 by Zeev Schiff. Schiff is a member of the
editorial board of Haorety, Israel's leading daily newspaper.

The book won the Soholov Prize as the outstanding
journalistic work of 1974. What separates this book from
most others is the author's ability to open files and give
verbatim extracts from the actual logbook records of the
fighting units. This allows the reader to derive more
primary material from this work than most other sources. The
book is very well organized. The author uses one day of war
per chapter except when he includes an "interlude" section on
some special subject of relevance to the day and chapter he
is about to or has just covered.

Trevor Dupuy wrote three books used in this study.
The first two, The Evalution of Weapons and Warfare, and
Numbers, Prediction, and War - Using History to Evaluate
Combat Factors and Predict the Outcome of Battles, are both
good background reading especially in conjunction with the
articles and reports prepared by his HERO (Historical
Evaluation and Research Organization) staff. His best work
is Elusive Victory which was published in 1978. Although the
book includes all of the Israeli-Arab conflicts to 1978, it
contains over 250 pages on the 1973 War. It is an excellent
source for several reasons. First, by 1978, a better
analysis could be made of the War. Some of the hasty
conclusions about the War were found to be myths. Dupuy is a
meticulous researcher and presents new evidence on certain
subjects. The author's objectivity is an asset not found in
many books published on the War. Depuy's reputation, as a
soldier-historian, opens sources that are unavailable to

others. The author's ability to research, analyze and

interpret the whole story makes this book very valuable.

Two other very objective books are, Insight on the

Middle East War and The Yom Kippur War. Both were written by

reporters of The Sunday Times (London). The two works

contain about the same material. The insight team covered in

detail the causes, preparation, tactics, and weapons used in

the War. They do not take sides and illustrate the successes

and failures of all combatants. The only problem is that the

books were written shortly after the War. It would be very

interesting to have the same writers go back to the

battlefield and again examine what took place to re-assess

their initial observations.

M.G. Chaim Herzog wrote two works covering the War,

The War of Atonement, October 1973, and The Arab-Israeli

Wars. The second book covers all the Middle East wars. The

section on the 1973 War is taken almost word for word from

his first book. It provides good background reading on the

events leading to the 1973 War. The War of Atonement,

October 1973 is an excellent account of the War but it does

not go into the depth of analysis of other works such as

those by Depuy. Also Herzog lacks objectivity. Some of his

criticism of Israeli leaders may be politically oriented.

The actual story of the fighting soldiers and day to day

details on both sides, is very good.

Two excellent case studies of the War were written

for the Air Force's and Army's Command and Staff Colleges.

The 1973 Mideast War from Air Command and Staff College
(ACSC) and Selected Readings in Tactics-The 1973 Middle East
War from the U.S. Army Command and General Staff College
(USACGSC), are exceptional background readings to understand
the day to day flow of the War. Both also have good
bibliographies and maps.

Theses

USACGSC theses are a good source of material. Most
of these were written just after the War or in the last few
years when many of the topics dealt with airland battle.
They provide a wealth of bibliographic information. The
majority of these studies were written by Air Force officers.
This gives a unique view to the value and deployment of the
air assets during the War.

"A-10 Effectiveness Against Soviet Offensive
Operations in Central Europe," by D.K Burke, uses experiences
of the Stuka pilots of the German Luftwaffe during World War
II and a few lessons from the 1973 War to illustrate the
requirements for a close air support aircraft in Europe.
Very little data can be gained from this thesis but excellent
insight on close air support (CAS) requirements makes it a
valuable source.

A USACGSC international student from Egypt, LTC
A.H.S. Hafiz wrote, "A Comparison Between US-Soviet Military
Doctrine from an Egyptian Point of View." It describes the
tactics used by Egyptian ground commanders during the 1973
War. It confirms the weaknesses of Soviet tactics that hurt

the Arab forces. The author is a veteran of the 1973 War.

Several studies completed in the last few years examined how the Air Force is going to perform the mission of BAI on the modern battlefield. "Close Air Support and Battlefield Air Interdiction in the Airland Battle," by David Hamilton, "The 'Air' in the Airland Battle," by J.R. Henderson Jr., "The Joint Airland Battle System: An Alternative to Air Ground Operations System," by H.R. Nichols, "Air Superiority Concepts: 1980-2000," by David E. Rickert, and "Close Air Support - Can it Survive the '80's?" by Ross L. Smith, are good references about how the Air Force plans to incorporate air support within the airland battle doctrine.

Two good historical sources are, "The Air Superiority Battle in the Middle East. 1967-1973," by C.E. Olschner, and "Airpower Theory and Application: An Historical Perspective," by Donald A. Streater. The first report provides excellent information about the air-to-air war and the use of air defense systems. The second covers World War II, Korea, and Vietnam but not the Middle East. It does point out the usefulness not only of studying history, but also of applying lessons from the past to doctrine of today and concepts for the future.

A 1985 thesis. "Tactical Airpower and the Rear Battle: Defeating the Operational Maneuver Group," by Albert Allenbach. is interesting because the problem of stopping the Soviet Operational Maneuver Group (OMG) 10-50 kilometers behind the friendly Forward Edge of the Battle Area (FEBA) involves many of the same problems as stopping a large reinforcing unit the same distance on the enemy side of the FEBA. Although the report is/shallow, the author provides a useful discussion of the value of changing the enemy's timing and tempo and how to do it.

Doctrine

The basis for airland battle doctrine is found in Field Manual(FM) 100-5, Operations (1982). This manual gives a general overview of airland battle and its components. It also serves as the capstone for a series of manuals that detail the specifics of doctrine for maneuver units, combat support and combat service support units. It stimulated the development of publications for joint service doctrine because of its emphasis on the use of airpower in the overall scheme of the ground commander. Among the more important Army manuals are: FM 6-20, Fire Support in Combined Arms Operations, FM 100-2-1, The Soviet Army-Operations and Tactics, FM 100-2-3, The Soviet Army-Troops, Organization, and Equipment, FM 100-15(Final Draft), Corps Operations and FM 101-5-1, Operational Terms and Symbols. Added to these Army manuals are Air Force Manual(AFM) 1-1, Functions and Basic Doctrine of the United States Air Force, Tactical Air Command Manual (TACM) 2-1, Tactical Air Operations, and USREDCOM Pamphlet 525-8, General Operations for Joint Attack of the Second Echelon.

These publications tell how the airland battle will

be fought by specific types of units. They establish
procedures to be followed. Unfortunately, they present only
generalized situations and can offer only a school solution.
Despite these shortcomings, they are the starting point of
the study and establish a set of boundries within which to
focus.

Periodicals

Most of the articles used were written either during
or just after the War. These give the initial impressions of
what took place but have little reflection about why. Some
articles published within the first few years after the War
are commentary on the War's outcome, specific phases of the
War, and weapons systems used. There was a period when
almost nothing was written in periodicals but with the
acceptance of airland battle doctrine, a resurgence of
analysis has occured, especially in Army publications.

The best source of immediate reactions concerning air
support is a series of articles appearing in Aviation Week &
Space Technology. The first articles, "The Mideast
Surprise," and "Soviet Aid Sparks Arab Gains," appeared in
the 15 October, 1973 issue only a week after the War started.
Both articles report the effectiveness of new weapons systems
such as the SA-6 anti-aircraft missile and the Saggar
anti-tank missile. The first article, an editorial, also
reminded the readers that in 1971, the journal reported the
missile belt along the Sinai. They had also noted that this
new air defense system changed the strategic balance of

airpower over the Suez Canal. The article reported that this
news was taken with great skepticism by Israel.

Other articles such as "Israeli Aircraft, Arab-SAMs
in Key Battle," "U.S. Spurs Countermeasures to Israel,"
"Mideast Cease-fire Spurs New Tensions," and "Israeli Losses
May Spur ECM Restudy," were published in the October issues.
They provide immediate impressions of weapons, tactics, and
mistakes on both sides. The evaluation of doctrinal changes
while the War was still going on is especially interesting,
as are impressions about the impact of new technology. This
last issue was stressed again in a November article, "U.S.
Equips Israel With Soviet Guided Weapons."

The next few months provided the initial articles
analyzing the airwar. December articles included, "The
Lessons of October," "Israeli Air Force Decisive in War, "
and "Egypt Assesses Lessons of October War." All three
articles covered the overall impact of the war in the air and
how the application of airpower changed during the course of
the War. They also reflect how the War may have changed
future doctrine.

The Journal of the Royal United Services Institute
for Defense Studies, which for the rest of the study will be
referred to as RUSI, published several articles in the early
years after the cea = fire which analyzed the conflict and
postulated a series of lessons learned from the War. These
articles, "Middle East Tank Fillers, " "The Middle East
War-An Assessment, " "Israel After the Yom Kippur War: Zahal

Reflects on the Lessons," and "The Assault on Mount Hermon:
an Episode of the October War," bring out information learned
from the War which is now incorporated in Israeli Defense
Force (IDF) doctrine.

The best article in RUSI is the text of a lecture
given to the RUSI staff on 6 November, 1974 by General Chaim
Herzog, former Chief of Israeli Military Intelligence. It
appeared in the March 1975 issue prior to General Herzog's
books on the War. The lecture is a good general overview of
the preparation leading to the War and its overall conduct.
One particularly interesting point is that General Herzog did
not try to coverup the intelligence failure of foreseeing the
attack by the Egyptians. Although the lecture does not
contain a lot on the day to day air activities, General
Herzogc makes several very important observations on the
usefulness of airpower and the effect of the dense Arab air
defense systems.

Military Review published several articles about the
War. Most of these were written in 1974 just after the War,
in 1976 when data from the War had been analyzed, and in 1978
in two specialized articles.

An excellent article, "The Yom Kippur War," appeared
in the March 1973 issue. The author, Kenneth S. Brower, gave
a complete overview of the War. He pointed out problems that
writers were going to have when analyzing the conflict.
Initial results from the battles led people to make hasty
conclusions. Upon deeper study of the final statistics from

the War, a different picture was formed. He gave the example

of the very high success rate of the IDF in 1967 and analysis

condemning their performance in 1973. Actually, loss rate

per 1000 sorties was less in 1973 than 1967.

In January 1976 S.L.A. Marshall submitted an article

from an anonymous author (probably Avigdor Kahalani) who was

a tanker on the Golan Heights front. It is very useful

because it describes the effects of enemy airstrikes on

armor. An interesting article, "The Syrian Side of the

Hill," was published in February. The author, Charles

Wakebridge, traveled to Golan and interviewed both sides,

including Syrian Defense Minister, General Tlass. It is

interesting to read the illusions of the Syrian high command

in their interpretations of the War. This is especially true

about the "success" of their Air Force.

An excellent article, "Israel's Defense Doctrine:

Background and Dynamics," by MG Israel Tal, Israeli assistant

minister of defense and deputy chief of the general staff

during the 1973 War, was published in March 1978. It gives

an overview of the IDF defense doctrine, strategy and

tactics. The author tells how these principles of defense

have worked through each Israeli conflict. The article

provides excellent background material and gives important

insight on why the IDF arms itself and why it uses specific

tactics to protect the country.

"The Sixth Arab-Israeli Conflict: The Military

Lessons for American Defense Planning," by Anthony H.

Cordesman, is found in the August 1982 issue of <u>Armed Forces</u>
<u>Journal</u>. It offers a good update of how the Israelis applied
lessons learned in the 1973 War to the invasion of Lebanon in
1982.

Two articles that give extensive coverage to the
airwar are "October War," from <u>Strategy and Tactics</u> and "Holy
Day Air War," from <u>Air Enthusiast International</u>. Both
sources provide a good overview of the airwar effects on the
outcome of the ground battle.

<u>Newsweek</u> is an important source of analysis and
on-the-spot reporting. Amaud de Borchgrave, senior editor,
traveled 800 miles in 24 hours in a taxi from Libya to Cairo
to start his reports and establish a team of reporters for
<u>Newsweek</u>. His personal relationship with President Sadat
allowed him more freedom than many journalists. His
extensive knowledge of the region, its leaders, and its
history, facilitated detailed analysis of the War.
Eyewitness reports from Nicholas C. Proffitt were also
informative and well written.

Most of the <u>Newsweek</u> articles are unsigned. They are
the day to day reports compiled in the weekly issue such as
"Tactics: How the Arabs Scored Their Surprise," "The Mideast
Erupts," and "Israel Scores a Breakthrough." Many articles
are about special subjects that related to the War like,
"Tank Warfare: World War I to West of Suez," "Restocking the
Arsenals," and "Five Lessons of the War."
<u>Reports</u>

Most of the reports were written by research firms under government contract. The majority were written within the first few years of the War. Most are classified but contain some unclassified data. Much of the classified data is found elsewhere in unclassified sources. The classified sources provide a good starting point for the search for data that is relevant and is usable if found in declassified sources.

An unclassified report by Martin von Creveld, Military Lessons of the Yom Kippur War: Historical Perspectives, was published by the Center for Strategic and International Studies in 1975. This excellent source, analyzes the weapons, tactics, and strategy of the War. The author's keen insight into what actually went on during the conflict makes this report valuable reading.

T.N. Dupuy's Historical Evaluation and Research Organization (HERO), produced a report, "Assessment of Arab-Israeli Conflict Effectiveness: 1973 War Combat Performance," for Mathematica, Inc.. It is an excellent source of statistical data concerning weapons, troop strength, etc. The firm uses a historical method to produce a formula for computing battle results. Through this formula, the reports give combat effectiveness ratios to each side. The significance of the reports, for this study, is the enormous amount of information on effects of weapons and detailed analysis of how certain battles were fought. Another report from HERO, "The Arab-Israeli War 1973," also provides good weapons data.

Two of the first unclassified reports completed by the Army are, "Lessons Learned from the 1973 Middle East Crisis," and "Air Defense in the Middle East," The first report, contains a separate section on air operations. This covers use of air controllers, the air-to-ground war, and air defense. The second report discusses Arab air defense systems both ground and air. It also relates how the initial effectiveness of these systems changed IAF support to ground forces.

A Department of Defense study, "The October 1973 Middle East War-Volume IV: Air Operations," and a Department of the Army study, "Analysis of Combat Data-1973 Mideast War Appendix E-Air Operations," are excellent sources. They were written shortly after the War and are classified. Most of the information in them is found in unclassified or declassified sources.

A report that confirms many of the problems associated with CAS is "The Fast FAC in Southeast Asia and its Utility in Future Conflicts." It examines the problems involved with controlling CAS near friendly forces in a high Threat air defense environment. Although the study is about Vietnam, it refers to the problems of the IAF in 1973. It confirms several facts about the actual percentage of use of CAS versus BAI.

Several reports use lessons from the 1973 War to illustrate future applications of airpower on the European battlefield. "Air Defense of the Covering Force in Central Europe," "Strategic and Doctrinal Implications of Deep Attack Concepts for the Defense of Central Europe," "Interdiction in Central Europe in the 1980's - An Analysis of Forces and Capabilities," and "An Assessment of the Impact of the October 1973 War on Soviet Doctrine, Tactics, and Material," all discuss the implications of the 1973 War on modern doctrine. A portion of each study is devoted to the importance of CAS or BAI and the problems of carrying out these missions in a highly developed air defense environment. With the similarities in tactics and weapons systems the 1973 War is used easily to project what may happen against Warsaw Pact forces. The problem is that most of the authors spend a great deal of effort relating the similarities but do not give enough analysis to the differences between the Middle East in 1973 and contemporary Europe.

Several good reports are found on the effect of air defense on the accomplishment of the air-to-ground mission during the War. "The Battle for Air Superiority during the 1973 Arab-Israeli War," "Defense Suppression," "Suppression in Support of Offensive Air Operations," and "Operational Methods Against Ground to Air AA Rockets as Conducted by the IAF," all express the view that the air-to-ground mission cannot be accomplished until the air-to-air and ground-to-air war is won or at least kept under control for limited periods. The reports give statistics on losses due to SAM's and interceptors. They also are informative about how the air defense systems were defeated or controlled to allow at least partial air support to ground forces.

Air-to-ground weapons effectiveness is of great concern to this study. Several reports are helpful in this area. "The Yom Kippur War: Analysis of Weapons Implications," is an excellent source not only of weapons data but it is also a good analysis of the total effectiveness of airpower during the War. "Middle East Game," from the U.S. Army Concepts Analysis Agency and "Historical Effects of Air Interdiction," describe the use of airpower in the 1973 War and its importance in stopping forces moving to the front. The reports analyze use of conventional air weapons against different types of targets such as tanks, trucks, and bridges. An excellent report on the damage done to tanks and personnel is "Value of Close Air Support." Although it was written to recommend the uses of CAS, it contains a section on airpower during the 1973 War with data from several studies.

One of the first reports about the War was written by S.L.A. Marshall for the Army Material Systems Analysis Agency. The report, "The October War - A Synopsis of the 1973 Sinai - Suez Campaign and a Critique of Weapons and Tactics," was published in January 1974. BG Marshall gave a good chronology of the War and then a preliminary analysis of what took place and why it happened the way it did. He evaluated different weapons systems and their uses. He believed one of the biggest influences on the War was the strong air defense. This thinking, that SAM's destroyed the IAF, is prevalent throughout most books, articles and reports written immediately after the War. It illustrates the caution an analyst must take when studying an event immediately after its completion.

Another excellent report, "31 January - 12 February (1974) Visit to the Israeli Defense forces," was published in March 1974 by TRADOC. It was written prior to the IDF publishing a report of lessons learned. The research staff got a feel for the initial lessons of the War by interviewing officers at all levels.

"The Israeli Air Force," was written for the Foreign Technology Division at the Air Force Systems Command. The report is very pro-IAF. It is a short chronology of the development of the IAF. Although a few facts are taken from the report, its lack of objectivity cloud the report's usefulness.

Newspapers

The newspaper is an excellent source of primary material. The papers examined were, The New York Times, The Times (London), and The Sunday Times (London).

The Sunday Times started an indepth series about the day to day fighting, tactics used, weapons systems, and advantages or disadvantages of each side. It had the luxury of being able to take a week's worth of reports from all the wire services and analyze them before going to press. The paper sent an insight team to Israel, Beirut, the United

Nations, Cairo, and Washington, to get a complete story on all the related events. This same team latter published their accounts in Insight on the Middle East War and The Yom Kippur War.

The Times (London) had reporters on each front as well as in Beirut. Each reporter was able to give personal reports of the fighting from the ground level but there was no analysis of what was going on or why. The overall coverage seems shallow. It may be due to leaving analysis to The Sunday Times.

Excellent reports can be found in the New York Times. The coverage is extensive on all fronts and in critical areas around the world. Here too a problem of balanced reporting existed although the accounts differ considerably. The reporter in Damascus, Juan de Onis, was limited to what could be sent and most of it was official statements of the Syrian government. Henry Tanner, at the Cairo desk, was allowed a little more freedom to visit the soldiers on the front lines. The best reports are from Terence Smith who covered the Golan Heights battle and was one of only three reporters to be allowed by the IDF to join their Sinai offensive to the west bank.

Expert analysis of the War came from Drew Middleton who had access to hundreds of stories coming over the wire services. Middleton is able to distinguish the true and meaningful stories and relate to the readers the significance of what takes place.

Newspapers are a good source of first hand information although they have little relevance to BAI. But, in a few articles, important on the spot reports on the effectiveness of airpower are found. The other benefit from this source is the analysis by The Sunday Times and Drew Middleton.

Chapter 3

METHODOLOGY

There are several advantages and disadvantages to
writing about a historical event that is only a little more
than ten years old. The major advantage is the number of
documents and personal observations that have been printed
and published. Unlike wars of the past, there is an
abundance of first hand writings from the soldiers who fought
the War, the generals who directed it, the politician who
caused it, and the people who paid for it. The major
disadvantage is that many reports are classified and can not
be used unless the information is found in an unclassified or
declassified source. Luckily, this was usually the case.
Several books published immediately after the War contained
information that later appeared in classified documents.
Another disadvantage is objectivity and limited views of the
writers. A participant in one phase of the War often wrote
as if he was everywhere on the battlefield.

Using historical methodology, this study examines the
following questions pertaining to the 1973 Middle East War:

1. The percentage of sorties used in BAI type missions.

2. The command and control of BAI.

3. The effectiveness of BAI.

4.   The types of targets that gave the best results.

5.   The problem areas that affected BAI.

The study is divided into five chapters. Definitions are placed in an appendix to enable a more informed reader to study the report faster and easier. Endnotes are used at the end of each chapter for ease of reading.

Chapter One is the thesis introduction. It presents the problem statement, purpose, research question, assumptions and significance of the study. It also establishes definitions that will be used and limitations of the study.

The review of literature in Chapter Two is designed to aid researchers studying similar subjects or considering the same sources. Most major sources are reviewed for their value to the study and support of the thesis research question. Where possible, several sources are examined together. All sources in the bibliography were analyzed in relation to the study though they may not appear in Chapter Two.

The methodology, Chapter Three, gives the reader a framework of how the study was performed and how it is organized. This is to assist the reader in his understanding of how the material in the study was derived.

Chapter Four covers the historical findings from the research. It first defines several key terms used throughout the rest of the paper. It is then organized into several chronological parts. The first part deals with the period

between the end of the 1967 Six-Day War and the start of the
1973 War. This was a very important period and the action is
written in detail because it covers the complete change of
Arab air defense systems, which had a major impact on the
air-to-ground war. This is also an important period because
of the influence of the super powers that helped shape the
air defense systems, doctrine, and tactics of each air force.

The pre-war events are followed by a short summary of
the ground war. This is necessary to understand what took
place during air-to-ground operations.

The airwar is the next section. It covers how and
when BAI was used, as well providing an evaluation of its
effectiveness. Also in this portion are the variables that
contributed to effectiveness of BAI such as the air defense
system, electronic warfare, and command and control.

Chapter Five, states the conclusions drawn from this
study. It discusses the NATO Central European scenario and
addresses how the conclusions of the thesis can affect future
air-to-ground support in that environment.

The research for the historical study began with a
comprehensive search through all services of the Combined
Arms Research Library of Ft. Leavenworth, Kansas. The
computer search of the Defense Technology Information Center
was especially useful. The library had 90% of all documents
needed either hardcover or on microforms. They were able to
provide most others within a few weeks. Some references were
unobtainable due either to being lost or destroyed.

While references were collected, the actual search for information about BAI took place. This was difficult at first because BAI was not a term used by either side and most of the initial studies are classified. After reading the reports, it appears that almost all the classified material could be found in articles and books. However, there is a void of any material written about the Arab countries airwar.

Another excellent source of information was interviews. The first was with Captain Ali Aklouche of the Algerian Army. CPT Aklouche did not participate in the 1973 War but has commanded a BMP battalion and is a graduate of two Soviet staff schools. His insight into the tactics and equipment used was very useful. The second interview was with COL. Doron Kadmiel, an artillery officer with the IDF. He was deputy commander of an artillery battalion in the Sinai during the War. His interview was very valuable to get the flavor of war and because the IAF CAS missions are controlled by artillery ground observers. He was also able to comment on the effects of Egyptian BAI on artillery positions.

This study uses the information collected to analyze the value of the BAI campaign during the War. It than draws conclusions as to its usefulness for the future.

CHAPTER 4

THE 1973 MIDDLE EAST WAR

Introduction

Before examining the role of BAI in the 1973 War, some common definitions must be established. Air Supremacy is the complete control of airspace to allow air operations to be conducted anywhere and anytime. Air superiority is the ability to gain contol of airspace at a specific place and time. It is usually held for a limited duration.[1] The Israeli Air Force uses almost the same definition of close air support as the U.S. Air Force. MG Binyamin Peled, Chief of Staff of the IAF during the 1973 War, states, "Close air support in our definition is that type of air-to-ground operation where a ground commander assesses his own situation, evaluates that he needs an air weapon to solve his immediate problems, calls for it."[2] In other words, CAS is called for in a local emergency at or behind the Forward Line of Troops (FLOT). The term battlefield air interdiction was not used by the IAF. The U.S. definition was stated earlier in this paper.[3]

Prelude to War

In 1973 the Israeli Air Force failed to play its proper role during the early days of fighting because events

34

prior to the War. For this reason, an explanation of the

pre-war period is critical to the study of the performance of

the battlefield air interdiction mission during the War.

Preparations for the 1973 conflict began shortly

after the 1967 Six-Day War. The foundations for planning,

tactics, and weapon systems were based on the results of the

outcome in 1967. The Arabs used their defeat to learn from

their mistakes and grow in their strategic and operational

level planning. The Israeli Defense Force (IDF) learned from

the War too. But, as is the case in many armies, they

trained for the 1967 War instead of the next one. The

lessons learned from the Six-Day War were modified by new

developments that occurred during the post-war period.

It seemed to most of the world that the 1967 Six-Day

War was a complete victory for Israel. The IDF killed or

wounded 68,000 Arabs, destroyed over 1,000 tanks, and

destroyed the air forces of Egypt, Jordan, and Syria. Israel

occupied 26,000 square miles of Arab land. This provided a

greatly increased defensive buffer and the complete

occupation of Jerusalem. All of this cost only 780 Israeli

dead and 2,600 wounded. The Israeli Air Force (IAF) lost

only forty-six aircraft, an almost ten to one margin of

damage compared to the Arab air forces. Also, the Israelis

made up for their losses in material with the capture of

enormous stocks from the Arabs.⁴ The balance of power in the

Middle East shifted radically in favor of Israel. For the

Arab countries it was a humiliating defeat.

The 1967 War gave little peace to Israel. Defeat only served to strengthen the ties among the Arab countries and confirm their will to destroy Israel. By flying a pre-emptive air strike against the Arabs on the first day of the War, Israel hoped to prevent a long costly war by destroying enemy military power quickly. They hoped this would force the Arabs to recognize the state of Israel and put an end to the state of belligerency that had existed in the region since 1948. Despite its impressive victory, Israel could not force the Arab nations to concede the goals it desperately wanted. The victory only antagonized the Arabs and weakened the influence of Arab moderates. The loss of sacred Arab national soil and numerous Muslim shrines made the Arabs even more determined.

Internationally, Israel's pre-emptive strike cost her major support among former allies. It also became a major factor in the 1973 War. The French condemned Israel for starting the War and put an embargo on war materials to Israel. President de Grulle stopped shipment of fifty Mirage fighter aircraft to the IAF even though they had been paid for in advance. The embargo also included parts. This hurt the IAF because the majority of its aircraft were French.[5] The War also helped to polarize the relations between the two superpowers. The Arabs, criticizing the U.S. for supporting Israel, turned to the Soviets for support. The Soviets, having supported and supplied arms to the Arabs for many years, seized an opportunity for further influence in the

region by strongly condemning Israel and starting an enormous
military aid program to the Arabs. Overall, the Six-Day War
created additional problems instead of accomplishing the
Israeli goals. Although, on the surface, Israel's victory
was impressive, it did not bring peace and served to create
the foundation for the next war.

The War of Attrition which followed, is probably the
least known and understood of all the Middle East wars. It
too had a great impact on the airwar in 1973. The War of
Attrition was a protracted series of raids, shelling,
terrorist attacks and air strikes on both sides of the 1967
cease fire lines. It was costly to the IDF in manpower (367
killed and 999 wounded) and was a drain on the economy. The
lessons of the War helped shape the Arab air forces.
Additionally, Soviet pilots took an active part toward the
end of the War.◆

Immediately following the 1967 cease fire, there was
an unparalleled degree of cooperation developed between the
powers of much of the Arab world, especially Egyptian
President Nasser, and the Soviet Union. Recognizing the air
superiority of the IAF, President Nasser let the Russians
have almost complete control over Egyptian air defenses in
hope of building up a counter-force to the IAF's domination
of the battlefield. The Soviets, who wanted to establish a
permanent presence in the region, were willing to make a
massive commitment to the Arabs. As a result, the Soviets
invested thousands of advisors and technicians, billions of

rubles worth of military hardware, and even the lives of some
of their pilots.

The Soviet buildup of the devastated Arab air forces
started immediately after the cease fire. By the
twenty-fifth of June, due to a massive Russian airlift, the
Egyptians had almost 200 aircraft. These new MIG-21s and
Sukhoi-7s gave the Egyptian Air Force (EAF) a more formidable
force than the one the Israelis destroyed.[7]

Because most of the Arab planes were destroyed on the
ground, they retained a sizeable nucleus of pilots. These,
plus new pilot candidates, were sent to the Soviet Union for
training.[8] The training they received was, by Western
criteria substandard. The Soviet training method of set
piece tactics was used. Manuals were written in Russian or
English that meant few pilots or crews had complete knowledge
of their aircraft. There was little training in air-to-air
or air-to-ground combat that did not fit into a set scenario.
Just prior to the 1973 War, flying time was curtailed to
conserve fuel, munitions, and aircraft. This meant a drop in
combat readiness before going into action against the
Israelis.[9]

As a result of the 1967 pre-emptive strike, the Arabs
learned that aircraft need to be dispersed and protected and
that their early warning system was inadequate. A new
program of runway improvement and hardened hangar
construction was started. They also requested a better radar
system from the Soviets.[10]

The IAF found huge obstacles in the way of their efforts to rebuild their Air Force. The French arms embargo became absolute on 4 January 1969. Since the air strike capability of the IAF was based on the French Mirage IIIC, this was a major set back. The U.S. took over the task of aiding the rebuilding of the IAF. The U.S. had supplied aircraft in the past but, for political reasons, these were not in great quantities. With the U.S. watching the massive Soviet buildup, President Johnson decided to send fifty F-4 Phantoms and some A-4 Skyhawks to Israel beginning in early 1969.[11]

The F-4 was a multi-role fighter with a Mach-2 speed and a 1000 mile combat radius. It performed about thirty-five to fifty percent in a ground role in 1973. The A-4 became the premier ground attack aircraft in the 1973 War. It was originally designed for carrier takeoffs. It was a single seat light attack bomber and it was extremely maneuverable. By 1971, The IAF had about seventy F-4s and eighty-eight A-4s.

The changeover from French to U.S. aircraft was a quantum leap for the IAF. The pilots and ground crews found the American aircraft simpler, yet more sophisticated more reliable, and better able to sustain damage and keep flying.[12]

The War of Attrition

Although the War of Attrition is generally considered to have started in the summer of 1969, it actually started a

few weeks after the cease fire. On 1 July, 1967, an Israeli
patrol was ambushed and cut off by Egyptian infiltrators.
This type of low level conflict continued on the Egyptian,
Jordanian, Syrian and Lebanese fronts until an August 1970
cease fire agreement. The War went through several phases,
from guerrilla war to dog-fights between Israeli and Soviet
pilots. The War had a single unifying theme in that, for the
first time, Israel had to fight a predominantly defensive
battle that would not be resolved by a decisive military
victory on the battlefield.[13]

The first aircraft to be shot down was an Egyptian
MIG-17 on 4 July, 1967. This was less than a month after the
cease fire of the Six-Day War. A week later, on 14 July, six
Egyptian MIG's and one Israeli aircraft were shot down during
a combined air and ground battle in the Suez area.[14]

Artillery shelling, commando raids, and deep
interdiction air strikes were continuous until the summer of
1969. Then the violence escalated. In May, eight MIG's were
shot down by IAF pilots and one was shot down by an American
made Hawk ground-to-air missile. Between the middle of June
and 7 July, the War escalated in all areas with nine Egyptian
planes shotdown.

One of the most decisive actions by the IAF occurred
on 17 June. It had a major impact on the Egyptian air
defense policy. Two IAF Mirages flew through the air defense
system at low altitude and high speed to Cairo where they
produced a loud sonic boom that shattered windows throughout

the prestigious suburbs of Manshieh el Bakri and Heliopolis.
As a result, Nasser fired both his air force and air defense
commanders. The raid also created a serious commitment to
rebuild the Egyptian air defense system.

Egypt began improving her air defense network in both
early warning devices and surface-to-air missiles (SAMs).
These latter were improved both in quality and quantity.
Egypt received SA2s before the end of the Six-Day War but
they were not operational prior to the cease fire. When the
Egyptians tried to move SAMs closer to the Canal, the IAF
bombed them before or shortly after they became operational.
On 25 December, in a continuous eight hour raid, the IAF
attacked and destroyed every missile battery from Quantara to
Suez City.

Additional raids and interdiction airstrikes against
an almost completely unprotected Egyptian airspace finally
forced Nasser to admit that the EAF could not protect Egypt.
On 22 January 1970, President Nasser flew to Moscow to stress
that Israel had achieved air supremacy and that massive
Soviet assistance in air defense would be needed. The
Russians were already aware of the Eygptian's
vulnerability.[18]

It was decided by the Soviets that the air defense
system would be rebuilt in stages. First, pilots and air
defense personnel continued to be trained while the Soviets
developed an extensive air defense plan. Then, a massive
airlift of new weapons (including SA3 missiles) arrived

starting in late January. The first systems were put around

Alexandria, with SA3s manned by Russians, to protect the

airlift that sometimes extended to as many as five transports

per hour. New MIG-21Js were then sent to Cairo piloted by

Russians. Ten squadrons, totaling 150 aircraft were

stationed at five different airfields.

By the end of March, the Soviets had installed a

completely new defense system for the Eygptians. An air

defense division was flown out of the Odessa air defense

district to the Western Egyptian delta region with its

headquarters in Alexandria. A forward air transport command

was headquartered in Cairo. MIG-21J and KSU-15 squadrons

were posted around Cairo and the Delta.

Now that Egyptian confidence was restored, they

increased the shelling along the Canal. The IAF flew deep

interdiction missions as well as BAI missions against

artillery emplacements.

On April 18, while flying south of Cairo, IAF pilots

heard Soviet voices on the radio and saw they were flying

against MIG-21Js instead of the Egyptian model. The pilots

broke contact and returned to home base. A new policy of

flying only in the air space around the Suez Canal was

established to avoid confrontation with the Russians who were

protecting Cairo.

By July, Soviet pilots were playing a major role in

the air defense of Egypt. They were actively challenging IAF

planes. On 25 July, two MIG-21Js flown by Russians, damaged an IAF A-4. This prompted Israel to retaliate. On 30 July they ambushed three flights of MIG-21Js. They downed five while sustaining damage to one of their own aircraft.

Shortly after this air battle, in August 1970, a United Nations cease fire went into effect. Egypt immediately started moving air defense batteries into the cease fire area. Between 7 August and 5 September, forty-five missile sites were constructed.[16]

The cease fire did not change the political or geographical situation in the Middle East. When Anwar el Sadat became president, he hoped to regain the lost Sinai. He prepared a treaty that ended the state of belligerence, recognized Israel's independence, and respected Israel's right to live within secure borders if Israel would return the Sinai. The Israelis refused, confident that their superior military power could retain the occupied territory. Trying to put pressure on Israel to negotiate, the U.S. cut off further shipments of aircraft. However, in January 1972, under pressure from pro-Israeli groups and with presidential and congressional elections approaching, President Nixon agreed to supply needed A-4s and F-4s to the IAF.[17]

Early in 1972, President Sadat began considering a limited military campaign against Israel to create an international crisis and thus to bring the superpowers influence to bear on Israel to give up lost Arab territory. Sadat knew he would need additional aircraft, missiles, and tanks from the Soviets who were unwilling to supply them due

to the questionable reliability of President Sadat. In July
1972, Sadat told the 21,000 Soviet advisors to go home.
Although this appeared to the world as a complete breakdown
of relations between the Soviet Union and Egypt, there were
still a large number of advisors and technicians who stayed.
In mid-November he decided to launch a campaign during 1973.

   Ironically, relations with the U.S.S.R. got better
and arms again flooded into Eygpt. Between December 1972 and
June 1973, Eygpt received more weapons than in the two
preceding years.[10] Along the Suez Canal, the Soviets helped
establish the most dense and comprehensive air defense
missile system in the world outside the Soviet Union itself.

   The most critical planning problem for the Egyptians
was how to avoid annihilation of their forces by the IAF
during the establishment of initial bridgeheads across the
Suez Canal. They knew they could control the air because
Israeli fighter-bombers had to come into the Egyptian air
defense belt to attack the bridges and follow on forces
supporting the crossing infantry. The Egyptians had faith in
their air defense umbrella.

   By the early 1970s, the Egyptian air defense network
was complete. The system, created for Egypt by their Soviet
advisors, was based on experiences from Vietnam and the
Middle East. The SA2, with its 30 kilometer range, was used
for high altitude aircraft and was supplemented with the SA3
which was faster and more agile. The SA6 was the primary
missile against low altitude aircraft. It was mounted on

mobile carriers and had the capability to change positions and radar frequencies. This made it hard to destroy or evade. The SA7 light anti-air missile was also abundant. It was carried individually or mounted on a vehicle with eight launchers. The missiles, along with thousands of anti-aircraft machineguns, radar controlled multi-barreled cannons, individual weapons, and of course the EAF, formed an almost impenetrable air defense umbrella.[19]

On the west bank of the Canal, the air defence sites operated as part of an integrated, mutually supporting network. They were protected by walls of earth and concrete and had anti-aircraft guns around them for protection against the IAF. Command and control elements were in underground bunkers. These supervised the integration of the missiles, guns, and fighter interceptors.

The typical missile site was a circular position of either SA2s or SA3s deployed in pairs. The command post was in the center of the position in a bunker. It was surrounded by the latest Soviet radar trailers. Around the site were decoy launchers made of wood. These made the identification of the real launcher very difficult. Outside the position, a network of multi-barreled anti-aircraft guns covered all approaches. The communications system was extensive throughout the air defense network. It consisted of radio and underground telephone cables. The SAM sites were integrated into a mutually supporting sector system controlled by a sector coordination site and equipped with

additional radars. About sixty sites were deployed along the
Canal in a strip 160 kilometers long and twenty kilometers
deep. Approximately one hundred other sites were dispersed
throughout the rest of Egypt to discourage deep interdiction
missions and air attacks against EAF airfields. The Arabs
regarded their missile network as a counter to IAF air
supremacy.

  During the War of Attrition, the IAF encountered many
missile sites, mostly SA2s, an were quite confident that
they could evade and destroy the missiles. But the Soviets
brought in new missiles, radars, and electronic systems that
rendered the previous IAF anti-missile tactics ineffective.

  In the final days of the War of Attrition, nine IAF
F-4s were shot down by the Egyptian missile system. The
message should have been clear to Israel that to gain air
supremacy, the Arab air defense belt must first be
destroyed.[20]

  By late 1972 the Egyptian Minister of War and
Commander-in-Chief, General Ahmed Ismail, had finished a
detailed plan for the Sinai campaign. It was based on
Egyptian strengths and Israeli weaknesses. The Egyptians
believed that Israel's major strengths were in airpower and
the rapid mobility of her armor. The Egyptians felt that
their Army was strong in a static defense because of their
larger manpower base. The Israelis could be defeated by the
attrition of their forces in attacks against Egyptian
defensive positions if the IAF was unable to support their

ground units or stop Egyptian reinforcements and supplies.
Also, a two front war would divide IDF military power.

The final Egyptian plan called for an attack across
the Canal on a wide front in order to deny the IDF the
ability to mass their forces at any one critical area. An
attack on a small front would have given Israel an ideal
target for air strikes while the Egyptians marshalled their
forces prior to and during the Canal crossings. Another
reason for attacking on a wide front was the placement of
Egyptian forces already defending along the Canal. If the
Israelis counterattacked along the wide front, the Egyptian
SAMs would be more effective against a lesser density of
aircraft. If the IAF tried to interdict only one or two
bridges, the Arab forces would still have many more bridges
available.

The plan called for a five infantry division attack,
each reinforced by an armored brigade. The divisions were to
attack in five major sectors, using numerous crossing sites,
and to establish bridgehead lines of about three miles wide
per division. The objectives were to seize the Bar Lev Line,
establish a defensive line within the SAM umbrella and defeat
Israeli counterattacks. The SAMs would, for the most part,
stay on the west bank out of artillery range. Once dug in,
the Egyptians felt they could strip away the IAF air support
from the attacking armor formations. They could then inflict
heavy losses on the IDF, and exploit the Israeli's limited
manpower and sensitivity to casualties. They felt that the

superpowers would intervene within the first few days to impose a cease fire and a negotiated settlement favorable to the Arabs. If this did not occur, the Arabs would engage in another war of attrition until /the IDF strength was so depleted that another attack could be launched to regain the rest of the Sinai.[21]

The Egyptians decided against attacking to secure the critical passes in the Sinai for several reasons. First was the limited EAF ability to support ground forces and carry out TAR. Second was the shortage of a mobile air defense network except for their SA6s and SA7s. Without an air defense umbrella, the IAF could interdict reinforcements and lines of communications (LOCs), while providing ground support to their own forces.

In January 1973, President Sadat was able to get President Assad of Syria to agree to join forces for Operation Badar (the code name for the attack) under an Egyptian commander. Although Syria was weaker than Egypt, the second front was needed to divide IDF forces, especially their air assets. Russia continued to supply Egypt and Syria with MIGs as well as significant amounts of the advanced and mobile SA6. Sadat also convinced Assad to abandon Syria's goal of destroying Israel in favor of simply recovering its lost territory. This would help the Arabs gain the superpowers' support during negotiations after the cease fire. The Egyptians and Syrians finalized plans for Operation Badar on 2 October with a decision to launch the attack at 1400 hours on 6 October.[22]

Like Egypt, Syria had been preparing for war since
1967. The Soviets supplied enormous amounts of military
equipment, especially SAMs which made up for Syria's lack of
interceptors and pilots. In May 1973, an agreement with the
Soviets provided Syria with a complete SAM defense system and
an additional forty MIG-21s.[23]

The Syrian plan, developed in conjunction with
Egyptians for an offensive on the Golan Heights, was to
attack with three mechanized divisions followed by two
armored divisions. The Syrian Air Force (SAF) would be used
immediately in a BAI role to stop reinforcement by closely
positioned units of IDF defensive positions along the border.
These positions would be sealed off, suppressed by a massive
artillery preparation, and then captured or destroyed by
Syrian ground forces.[24]

In contrast to the Arabs, the IDF did not learn as
much from the Six-Day War. Their total victory gave them a
defensive buffer area and a sense of complacency. They
developed an inflated estimate of their own power and an
unrealistic opinion of Arab military proficiency and
capabilities. This attitude was expressed by General Ariel
Sharon shortly after the end of the war in 1967 when he said,

> After our success this time, I am very much afraid
> that by the time of the next war we are all going
> to be too old, and the next generation will have
> to take care of it, because...the enemy is not
> going to be able to fight for many, many,
> years.[25]

In analyzing the 1967 War, the IDF attributed their success to better planning, generalship, and manpower. They concluded that the combination of air support and armored power appeared to be the foremost cause of their victory. They failed to analyze what would have happened if they had not had air supremacy. They failed to evaluate the major effect that the IAF had both physically and psychologically, on Arab ground forces. The IDF's greatest success came after they achieved air supremacy. It is not surprising then, that during the period between wars the IDF devoted most of their defense spending to strengthening their Air Force and armored forces. Over seventy-five percent of their defense budget went to these two branches, with over fifty percent going to the IAF alone.[24] It was decided that infantry and artillery would only play a secondary role. The Air Force would be used as flying artillery with the ability to bring much more fire power to bear on the enemy than cannon field artillery. Flying weather in the Middle East was so good that artillery would only have to fire at night when the IAF did little flying.

After the Six-Day War, it was assumed that the IAF could gain aerial supremacy at any time over the Arabs, serve as the strategic arm of the IDF, and give full support to the ground attack. Israeli defense plans were built around the speed and lethality of the IAF. It was the main force multiplier. The War of Attrition only served to strengthen these beliefs. The Egyptian missile build up at the end of 1970 was considered minor.[27]

Along the Suez Canal the IDF plan of defense was based on a widely spaced series of defensive positions along the Canal, called the Bar Lev Line. The strongpoints of the Bar Lev Line were safe from shellfire and did not require many troops. These positions were not designed to fight against even light attacks. They were designed for observation and requesting fire support to delay the enemy until reinforcements arrived. The infantry manning them had only small arms, machineguns and light anti-tank weapons.[28] The IDF felt they could be supported by artillery in two minutes and with armor in ten to twenty minutes. This would blunt the attacks while the IAF flew ground support missions against enemy troop concentrations.

In the Sinai the Israeli strategic defensive positions were located along a line roughly parallel to the Canal and fifty to sixty kilometers east of it. The positions controlled the Khatmia Pass, Giddi Pass, and the Mitla Pass. There are four major roads across the Sinai. The three passes control east-west movement along the central, southern and south eastern routes.[29]

On the Golan Heights, Israel did not have a large buffer like the Sinai nor were their defensive positions as elaborate. If the Syrians broke through the initial defensive belt, their next objective would be to cross the Jordan River. If they crossed the River, they could drive through the heart of Israel.

A major part of the overall defense plan was an IAF pre-emptive strike into Arab territory to halt units moving to crossing sites, destroy enemy airpower, and support ground forces. Due to the reliance on the pre-emptive airstrike, the first IAF priority was to create narrow corridors in the Arab air defenses through which the IAF could fly to attack their targets. This was planned for in two ways. One way was to use ground forces to cross the Canal to destroy SAM sites and forward airfields. The other plan was for the IAF to attack the SAM sites in a less densely covered corridor.[30]

The Arabs were now ready for war. They believed their air defense systems would stop the IAF from supporting ground elements and from preventing Arab reinforcements from building a massive attacking force. They knew their air forces were not prepared to do battle with the elite of Israel's military power, the IAF pilots. Arab planes would be used for initial surprise BAI and interdiction strikes behind the forward edge of the battle area (FEBA) against tank parks, reserves, command and control elements, airfields, and supply depots. The air forces would then return to bases deep in their own territory to play a secondary air defense role. Very little air-to-ground support would be available to Arab ground commanders.

Israel had complete trust and faith in its Air Force. In 1971, an IAF spokesman stated:

We are convinced we have the full answer to
missiles. In July 1970, we didn't have it. Now
there will be no serious problems. There will be
losses, but smaller than those we sustained on the
eve of the cease fire [War of Attrition]. This
should be proven within the first two or three
hours of war. We will overcome the whole system
within two or three days.[31]

Because Israel believed the missiles were vulnerable
to a concerted effort, they felt the fight for air supremacy
would be won primarily in air-to-air combat over the inferior
Arab Air Forces. In 1973, Israeli intelligence estimated
that the Arab air forces would not be a serious threat for
several years. Without an effective counter to IAF air
supremacy, Israel believed any Arab ground attack would be
destroyed by its Air Force. This over confidence in airpower
caused Israel to misinterpret intelligence data on the
upcoming war.[32]

Pre-War Summary

The period between the Six-Day War and the 1973 War
is important to the study of BAI for several reasons. First
the development of the Arab air defense system took away the
IAF air supremacy. This lead the Arabs to believe that they
could attack Israel without the IAF destroying their ground
forces. The airpower balance had changed. This opened the
door for war. Second, as the Arabs changed their plans to
overcome their weaknesses, Israel reinforced what appeared to
have given them victory in 1967. The IDF plans were built
around the assumption that the IAF could destroy Arab air

forces rapidly, without worrying about being shot down, prior

to supporting the IDF ground attack. They also failed to

adjust to a change in Arab tactics that would cause the IAF

to initially fail in the ground support mission. Third,

during this the period time superpowers made their full

commitments to their client countries. This not only changed

the balance of air supremacy as the Soviets built up the Arab

air defense systems, but also helped change the IAF by

converting it to American planes. This commitment, latter in

the War, also kept the conflict going longer because of the

massive resupply efforts by both superpowers.

TABLE I

AIR ORDER OF BATTLE, 6 OCTOBER 1973

	EGYPT	SYRIA		ISRAEL
FIGHTER-BOMBERS				
SU-7	130	45	A-4	150
MIG-17	200	120	F-4	140
MIG-19	60	--	SUPER MYSTERE	12
MIG-21	<u>160</u>	<u>110</u>	MIRAGE	<u>50</u>
	550	275		352
BOMBERS				
TU-16	18	--	VAUTOUR	8
IL-28	<u>30</u>	--		
	48			
SAM LAUNCHERS				
SA-2/3	800	300	HAWK	75
SA-6	80	60		
SA-7	<u>920</u>	<u>532</u>		
	1,800	892		
AA GUNS				
ZU-23	450	258	20-MM	770
ZSU-23-4	300	184	40-MM	<u>212</u>
57MM	<u>550</u>	<u>294</u>		982
	1,300	736		

<u>Source</u>: Historical Evaluations and Research Organization
(HERO), "The Arab-Israeli October War, 1973," <u>Combat Data
Subscription Service</u>, Vol.2, No.2, Spring 1977, pp. 3-7.[33]

Opening Moves

On the fourth of October, the Israeli Air Force found very strong evidence of an Egyptian intent to attack during examination of film from special TAR flights along the Canal. It was evident that bridging and water crossing equipment was being positioned along the Canal.

Early on the fifth, the films were shown to the head of the IDF military intelligence, the Defense Minister and the Chief of Staff. It was decided that a higher state of alert would be enacted but mobilization was not started. The IAF was so alarmed by recent reports that it made a telephonic call-up on the fourth. This was possible because of the small number of reservists in the IAF.[34]

The decision not to mobilize had drastic effects on the IAF although it had most of its manpower ready for duty. Complete mobilization takes seventy-two hours to expand the IDF from 80,000 to 300,000 personnel. Because the Army was not mobilized, the IAF had to allocate a larger percentage of its sorties to CAS and BAI support to compensate for the lack of reserve armor and artillery that were not at the front.[35]

From intelligence data, analyzed over a two week period, a message was sent to the Chief of Staff, David Elazar, at 0400 hours on the sixth, that war was eminent and that the Syrians and Egyptians would attack at 1800 hours that evening. At 0800 hours, Defense Minister Moshe Dayan,

Elazar, and Prime Minister Golda Meir met to discuss their options. Besides total mobilization, Elazar wanted a pre-emptive strike. Dayan disagreed with a pre-emptive strike. Meir ordered a mobilization but no airstrike. Meir and Dayan worried about world opinion, especially that of the United States. Another consideration for not allowing the pre-emptive strike was that the world would now see that Israel needed the buffer area it captured in 1967, separating it from the Arab nations, for its own preservation.[36] Also, the military balance was different now than in 1967. In the Six-Day War, total IAF resources were used in the pre-emptive strike to destroy Arab planes on the ground. Now, with the new radars and missiles, a large part of the IAF had to be used for SAM suppression and planes would be lost. The effects of the 1967 airstrike would not have the same results. The IAF could not destroy the Arab air forces, control the skies with limited planes, and then turn the vast majority of their sorties to ground support. BAI sorties would now have to be flown into areas where the IAF did not have air superiority. But, Israel felt it would not take long to destroy the Arab missile belt.

Since the decision was made not to fly a pre-emptive strike, the IAF planned to launch a counter-air campaign on the morning of the seventh. Approaching darkness on the sixth at 1800 hours, the given time of the Arab attack, precluded effective counter-air strikes.[37]

The Ground War

The War began sooner than the Israeli intelligence
anticipated. On the southern front, Egyptian fighter-bombers
crossed the Suez Canal at 1405 hours on the sixth on their
way to bomb Israeli airfields, headquarters, tank parks,
reserve motor pools and supply areas. Over 2,000 guns
started firing simultaneously on the Bar Lev Line. During
the barrage, 8,000 troops crossed the Canal in rubber boats,
bypassed the IDF strongpoints, and moved three to six miles
east to set up a defensive position. Commandos were also
sent east to set up ambush positions to slow the movement of
reserve forces to the front. The capture of the strongpoints
was left up to the second and third echelons.

By 2200 hours, the Egyptians had cut gaps in the sand
wall of the Canal bank and had six bridges across the Canal.
They continued rafting and bridging operations all night in
support of the buildup of their defensive positions.

Within twenty-four hours, most of the strongpoints
were captured and local counterattacks were beaten back. The
Egyptian perimeter consisted of a large number of anti-tank
guided missiles, anti-tank guns, and tanks. The Israelis,
denied air support by the Arab air defense system,
counterattacked with their armor. Since they were within
enemy artillery range, did not advance with their infantry,
and had very limited artillery of their own, their attacks
caused heavy losses without breaking the Egyptian line.

The front stablized by the tenth. While Egypt was
planning their next offensive action, IDF General Sharon was

scouting Canal crossing sites that he built three years prior to the War. He wanted to attack across the Canal immediately but was told to wait until more Egyptian armor crossed to the east bank which would give his attack, Operation Gazelle, a better chance of success.

The Egyptian offensive began on 14 October with an assault by 1,500 tanks. This time, the Arabs did not have their air umbrella to hide behind because it had not displaced forward. They were stopped and turned back with the loss of over 200 tanks.

Sharon was now given permission to begin Operation Gazelle. After hard fighting by Sharon's force, a bridgehead was formed. Although the Egyptians first thought the crossing was only a raid, they soon realized it was a major attempt to encircle them. They attacked the bridgehead on the west bank sending elements of two divisions south. One brigade was ambushed losing twenty-six tanks. The other armor units failed to cut off the corridor across the Canal.

The Israelis on the west bank began overrunning SAM sites which allowed for IAF support. Sharon moved to threatened Ismailia. The divisions of Generals Magan and Aden crossed through Sharon's bridgehead and turned south toward Suez City to cut off the Third Egyptian Army. Although part of the Egyptian force was cutoff, the Second Army was entrenched and the IDF could not break their hold in the Sinai. But, the Egyptians could not move forward. Even though both sides were receiving massive resupplies from the superpowers, they were exhausted. A cease fire went into effect on 24 October.

On the northern front, the Syrians started their attack at the same time as Egypt. Their offensive started with a massive armor force supported by airstrikes and an artillery barrage. The two IDF brigades on the Golan Heights fought a series of tank battles against as much as twelve to one odds. They were pushed back to the 1967 cease fire line.

The IDF's first priority was the Golan Heights because there was little room there for withdrawal into Israel. The Sinai offered a larger area in which to fallback. The majority of mobilized reserves, supplies, and firepower was sent against the Syrians during the first days of the War. By the tenth of October, the Israelis had pushed the enemy back to their original positions. The battle cost both sides heavily. Every Israeli tank on the line on the first day of fighting was hit. The Syrians lost over 800 tanks within Israeli territory.

Now it was time for the IDF to attack. On the eleventh, a two division operation was launched toward Damascus. Both Iraqi and Jordanian units were sent to stop the advance. Although large numbers of Arab forces were destroyed, they could not stop the IDF until the fourteenth when the advance was finally halted short of Sasa. However, Damascus was in range of Israeli 175mm guns and was continually shelled. Also, on the twenty-first, the IDF was able to recapture Mount Hermon which was lost to the Syrians on the first day of the War. The cease fire followed.[38]

Air-To-Ground Operations

Operation Badar started four hours earlier than IDF
intelligence predicted. In the Sinai, Egyptian artillery
fired a twenty minute preparation on the Bar Lev Line at 1405
hours to start the War. Simultaneously, a coordinated
airstrike with approximately 220 Egyptian planes sought
revenge for the 1967 IAF pre-emptive strike by attacking
airfields at Bir Gifgafa, Bir el Thamada, Ras Nasrani,
Ophira, El Arish, Akaba, and Ras Sedar. Their aim was to
strip away Israeli air cover and ground support aircraft.
More strikes were directed against forward command and
control facilities at Tasa and Bir Gifgafa along with eight
to ten Hawk air defense batteries. BAI strikes were flown
against artillery batteries and reserve positions.[39] More
sorties were flown against electronic monitoring and jamming
stations near Om Khushaib and Om Morgan. Other air
operations tried to close roads leading to the front and
supply depots. The EAF admitted the loss of ten aircraft.
Israel says it shot down sixteen Egyptian planes.[40]

The EAF was very well prepared for the air offensive.
Many target replicas were built in Libya for rehearsals. The
strikes were carried out without much opposition from the IAF
or Hawk air defence batteries. Losses of Egyptian aircraft
were light considering that the IAF was on full alert.
Whether the inability of Israel to react to the air strikes

was due to surprise or because they were loaded for their pre-emptive strike is unknown.[41]

Because of the distance between the two fronts, the lack of artillery, and the slowness of the armor reserve, the IAF was the only possible tactical reserve that could be used to stop the attack. Because of this, the IAF had to abandon their normal policy of clearing enemy air defense systems prior to supporting ground operations. Also, pilots sacrificed the use of counter measures against the air defense systems for faster direct attacks on the crossing forces. This caused heavier losses than anticipated. Not only were the attacks flying directly into the air defense system, but the numbers, tactics, and coordinated effort of the Egyptian air defense forces caught the IAF surprised and unprepared.[42]

The IAF's F-4 Phantoms and A-4 Skyhawks were in action within twenty-six minutes from the first reports of the Egyptian crossings. Their attempts to stop the crossing were frustrated by the new comprehensive air defense system. They were forced to fly low to stay away from the SA2s and SA3s. This put them in range of the ZSU-23-4s, SA6s, and SA7s.[43] The IAF losses mounted rapidly. The ground support promised to the maneuver forces did not come close to what was requested.

The Egyptians were surprised at how easy the crossing was. They expected thousands of casualties but only had 180 dead in the first wave. The bridgehead on the west bank was packed with vehicles and troops waiting to cross the bridges, an excellent BAI target. But, the IAF could not attack the targets without a high risk of being shot down. During the afternoon, an IDF general told his officers, "If only I had more artillery."[44] Israel was paying a high price for basing its fire support on airpower and neglecting the field artillery. Targets that were attacked by air were limited to one pass. This was not considered effective.

Field artillery was used to try to fill the airpower void. The artillery became over committed for its numbers and ammunition supplies. Due to the heavy volume of Egyptian artillery and accuracy of their counter-battery radar, Israeli artillery became heavily engaged by the Arabs. Many batteries were required to move twenty minutes after occupation of a new position or risk being targeted. Egyptian forward observers were also sent behind Israeli lines to call in fire on IDF batteries.[45] Little fire support reached the troops on the Bar Lev Line.

One of the most significant developments of the War was that the IAF did not have air supremacy as in previous wars. They could not fly ground support until the SAMs were destroyed without risking a high lose rate. Appalled by the losses, the Israeli Chief of Staff suspended all air operations just after 1600 hours. Because the urgency for ground support and a rapidly deteriorating situation, he sent the IAF back into the air about an hour latter.[46]

Although shocked by the Egyptian air defense belt and

the knowledge that their effectiveness would not be as planned, the IAF made repeated attacks on both sides of the Canal. Egyptian arm   units, vehicles and troops were attacked at Port Said. Second echelon forces attacking strongpoints were attacked as were a few missile sites. Israel claims to have hit ten of the bridges across the Canal within the first twenty-four hours of the War. The IAF believe that Egypt lost thirty-seven planes downed in air battles or by Israeli anti-aircraft fire.[47]

The Egyptian Army tried to cross the Canal with twenty commando battalions to seize crossroads and passes, destroy command and control facilities, and stop reinforcements moving to the front. In effect, the commandos were trying to perform some of the same functions as BAI. Throughout the War, commando raids were substituted by the Arabs for a lack of BAI effort since the EAF was afraid to fly out of their air defense belt. Israel also used commandos to make up for a lack of BAI at night or in coordination with BAI. An Egyptian raid the first night suffered heavy casualties with loss, according to the Israelis of eight helicoptors.[48]

The major effort of the IAF the first day was in the Sinai in a BAI role. The IAF flew approximately 200 sorties before dark. They lost five A-4s and one F-4.[49]

The second day of the War began for the IAF at 0645 hours when their aircraft made a number of preparatory strikes against the missile system before coming in for ground support missions. Due to the deteriorating situation on the Golan Heights, the mission priority of effort was directed to the northern front.[50]

At 1400 hours, in another shift of command direction, a considerable number of sorties were launched against the Suez Canal bridges. They were not easy targets because the aircraft had to approach from the west bank because of the high berm of sand on the east bank. The west bank, of course, was packed with guns and missiles. Two A-7s were shot down during these attempts to destroy the bridges.[51] Additional missions were directed in support of the Bar Lev strongpoints still holding out along the Canal.[52]

The Egyptian Air Force continued with its limited air attacks and additional helicopter raids on the seventh. At 1200 hours, the EAF claimed to have raided targets in the Sinai and attacked near Bir Gifgafa in the late afternoon. Several attacks around 1400 hours were directed against strongpoints and various targets near Baluza with forty SU-7, MIG-17s and MIG-21s.[53]

EAF attacks on ground targets continued on the eighth. Sorties were flown against targets that included air bases, Hawk batteries, radar stations, and reserve armor units moving to the front.

From the eighth through the thirteenth of October, the IAF continued significant air activity on the Sinai front. Again on the eighth, raids struck at the Egyptian bridges and damaged several. Airstrikes were started against

military targets in the Port Said area to stop attempts to
send reinforcements from the north and to keep
ground-to-ground missiles out of the area.[54] Also on the
eighth, aircraft missions were flown in support of ground
attacks in the northern sectors with about twenty-four
sorties carried out around the Fridan bridge. Air-to-ground
coordination was poor and some Israeli aircraft attacked
their own Natke brigade.[55] On the ninth, the IAF attacked an
Egyptian armor advance in the the south towards Ras Sudar,
beyond the covering Egyptian air defenses. It was severely
damaged by Israeli aircraft in support of the defending
paratroopers. Later in the day, Israeli leadership again
directed the priority of effort towards the Golan front in
support of an Israeli offensive.[56]

          The EAF flew limited attacks between the ninth and
thirteenth. Missions they flew were low level attacks by
small numbers of aircraft which remained behind the air
defense umbrella.

          The following is an account by an Israeli of BAI attacks
in his area during the early days of the War.

          A painful event occurred that day in my sector.
          In a show of daring, the Egyptians dispatched
          planes that carried out short, low altitude
          sorties over our lines. Two of these planes hit a
          point on the Ma'adim Road where four tanks from
          one of Nate's battalions were reloading with
          ammunition; two platoon leaders were killed and
          crewmen were wounded. At 1400 hours two other
          enemy aircraft bombed a point that was some 15
          kilometers east of the front line, on the Ma'adim
          Road. This was a working site for one of our
          forward ordnance companies, repairing tanks. Fuel

tanks were there also, as well as vehicles loaded
with ammunition and nearly two hundred men....The
men overconfidently thought that our air force was
in control of the skies and that the Egyptians
would not dare send their planes into our
territory. This was a serious miscalculation, and
we paid dearly for it: fuel trucks caught fire,
ammunition began exploding all around, and eighty
of our men were wounded.[87]

On the fourteenth, the Egyptians tried to expand
their bridgehead. The EAF flew support into the Sinai
against forces moving to stop their advance. Deeper attacks
were again directed at Hawk missile batteries and electronic
jamming stations to the rear of the front lines commencing at
0615 hours.[88] This was an attempt to open corridors to let
ground support sorties fly without concern of being shot down
by Israeli air defense weapons. The ground support sorties
began at 0620 hours with Egyptian aircraft carrying out
attacks to support the divergent drives of the armored
forces. These were generally brief attacks with no
appreciable impact on the battlefield. The commandos were
countered by Israeli paratroopers.[89]

The IAF reacted powerfully to the Egyptian offensive
on the fourteenth. One Egyptian tank column penetrated
twelve miles to the Mitle-Ras Sudan road where they were held
up by Israeli paratroopers. Israeli aircraft attacked and
severely damaged the column. Within two hours of the opening
of the offensive, Israeli aircraft accounted for sixty
Egyptian tanks and a large quantity of armored personnel
carriers and artillery.[90] By this time replacement of

Phantoms and Skyhawks began to arrive from the United States along with resupplies of ammunition and other ordnance.

The Israeli plan to cross the Canal was feasible due to the ability of the IAF to switch their priority back to the Sinai front. The IAF vigorously supported the crossing effort as well as the battles, such as the Chinese Farm, that led up to the advance into Egypt. On the evening of the sixteenth, reinforcements arrived near the Chinese Farm including an airborne battalion brought in by helicopters. On the morning of the seventeenth, frequent air attacks were delivered against the Egyptian units of the 25th Armored Brigade which were moving north on artillery road against the Israeli corridor separating the Egyptian armies. Additional air support was delivered as the Israelis methodically pounded the Egyptian positions around and to the north of the Chinese Farm.[41] The forces on the west bank of the Canal fanned out and destroyed missile batteries creating a fifteen mile wide SAM free corridor. Israeli pilots quickly adopted new tactics. The Israeli ground attack aircraft approached very low over the Sinai, climbed to gain height in the area of airspace now cleared of surface-to-air missiles, then dove to create a wall of rocket and cannon fire for the Israeli forces around the perimeter of the bridgehead. For the first time, Israeli ground commanders could count on the IAF clearing positions well ahead of their advance. The Egyptians on the west bank again faced the classic Israeli combination of armor and airpower. Slowly, the Egyptians were overrun or retreated as the bridgehead expanded.[62]

The withdrawal and destruction of the Egyptian missile batteries opened up the skies for the Israelis during the final days of the War. Starting on the nineteenth, armor forces, advancing south to encircle the Egyptian Third Army, received the best air support of the War. The airfield of Fayid fell affording the Israelis an important airhead that was used for resupply.[63]

For the rest of the War on the Sinai front, the IAF enjoyed almost complete air superiority which again allowed them to support the ground forces without the losses they had experienced during the first days of the War. The rapid gains and light losses associated with the final offensive drives of the Army highlighted a professional display of combined arms tactics much like that of 1967.[64]

A period of Egyptian air inactivity followed until the Israeli attacks across the Canal. Major efforts by the Egyptians were mounted against the IDF forces during the battle of the Chinese Farm on the sixteenth and then in the battle to stop Israeli advances into Egypt from the seventeenth through the nineteenth. On the seventeenth, the EAF attacked the Israeli Canal crossings sites and pontoon barges ferrying tanks across the Canal. In the most concentrated attack so far, rockets and bombs hit one of the ferries making it inoperable. The attacks on the crossing sites came in waves. Each wave was made up of jets and helicopters attempting to bomb the bridges and ferries. By the last attack, late on the afternoon of the eighteenth, despite crippling losses, damage was inflicted upon the bridge.[44]

On the nineteenth, because of the serious threat posed by the Israeli bridgehead, the Egyptian Supreme Command committed most of the air reserve to the fight. As in previous days, the EAF attacked in waves with SU-7 and MIG-17 fighter-bombers protected from above by MIG-21 Fighters.[45] Throughout the 19-24 October period, large numbers of fighters attempted to interfere with the ground support being flown by the IAF. Air defense efforts by the Egyptian forces did interfere with this support to some extent, but Egyptian air-to-air losses were severe.[46]

On the northern front, the Syrian Air Force started the War exactly like the Egyptians, with a large coordinated air strike. Almost one hundred Syrian planes took part in the initial attacks which were directed at Israeli command posts, observation posts, artillery positions, armor track parks, and fortifications. Principal targets were the observation positions on Mount Hermon and the command and control headquarters at Naffak. The main purpose of the strikes was to delay and disrupt IDF attempts to get their forces to the front before the massive Syrian armor attack could overrun the IDF positions. The SU-7 and MIG-17 fighter-bombers came in very low while MIG-21 fighters provided cover from IAF fighters. Some of these aircraft tried to penetrate into the Huleh Valley but were reportedly

driven off by Israeli Hawk fire.[47] Israeli interceptors
interfered with these initial strikes very little.

The necessity to conduct simultaneous air combat
operations on the Golan front, while combat raged in the
Sinai, caused heavy additional demands on the IAF. On a
number of occasions these critical demands were met by
shifting the emphasis of air operations from one front to
another. This did not mean that a particular front was
stripped of aircraft, but rather a prioritization of sorties
available went to the front with the most fighting. Because
of the initial ground gained by the Syrians and the lack of
terrain in which to defend, the Israeli priority after the
confusion and surprise of the sixth was initially directed
toward Syria.

On the Golan Heights, Israeli reaction to the Syrian
advance mirrored that in the Sinai. Like the southern front,
initial airstrikes flew into the SA6 and intense
anti-aircraft artillery fire. Ground losses rose quickly
during the suspension of airstrikes. Upon their renewal the
Israeli aircraft adopted the tactic of a low altitude, high
speed approach to the north over Jordanian territory with a
quick pop-up over the Golan plateau to strike the Syrian
armor from the flank and curve away west of Mount Hermon.
This was partially successful and air losses were reduced.

Due to the all night advance of the Syrian armor, the
situation was again critical on the morning of the seventh.
The airborne pounding began at dawn with successive waves of

Phantoms and Shyhawks streaking across the Heights firing rockets, cannons, and dropping bombs against the Syrian columns. The missiles and dense anti-aircraft fire wreaked havoc. For example, in the area of Juheder, an Israeli battalion commander asked for air support at first light. As the sun rose, four Skyhawks penetrated to bomb the Syrians, but as they approached their targets the tell tale smoke trails of the SAMs were seen. All four planes exploded in the air in full view of the hard pressed troops of the battalion. Undeterred, a second flight of four attacked and two exploded.[48] The intermingling of forces made identification of ground targets difficult and CAS impossible. At the same time additional strikes were directed specifically at Syrian air defenses. By 1500 hours, the Syrian thrust was halted but with heavy aircraft losses. Attempts by Syrian fighters to support their ground forces on the seventh had little effect on the battle since the IAF had air superiority in areas outside the Syrian air defense screen.

The extremely heavy Israeli air attacks during the first few days of the War were not only directed at the Syrian ground penetrations, but also at the SAM batteries and supporting anti-aircraft artillery positions themselves. Initially, the air defense forces were very successful against the Israeli attacks, extracting a high toll of Israeli aircraft. As was the case with the Egyptians, when the Syrian ground forces attacked outside their air defense umbrella, the level of protection fell.[69]

On the eighth of October, Israeli Phantoms raided the Omer, Halhul, Nasseriya, and Seikal air bases around Damascus while intensive efforts continued against the Syrian ground forces on the Golan.

The Israelis executed a counter offensive from the ninth to the thirteenth. In preparation for the offensive, the Air Force attempted to clear the area north of Hushnizal of SAM batteries. The Israelis concentrated their efforts into one of the heaviest raids against the Syrian air defense barrier. Ninety-five aircraft attacked and by the end of the day heavy smoke was observed over fifteen batteries.[70] In addition, on the ninth and tenth, a series of deep strikes penetrated into Syria. In one raid six Phantoms appeared over Damascus and bombed a half dozen buildings including the Ministry of Defense, Syrian Air Force headquarters, a radio station, the city's power station, and, by accident, foreign embassies. Other raids struck oil storage tanks and electric power generators at Homs. The fuel tanks and loading facilities at Adra, Tartous, and Lalakia were bombed as well as the Mediterranean terminal for Iraqi crude oil at Baniyas. Additionally, raids destroyed the computerized control center for the Syrian air defense network, and two Phantoms attacked the radar station on the 7000 foot high Barouch Ridge in Lebanon.[71] On the tenth, Israeli aircraft stuck deep into Syria again aiming at airbases including those at Habeb and Damir. These attacks on airbases continued on the eleventh

73

as did more strikes against other economic targets.[72] Large
air battles occurred during the strikes and also during the
Israeli ground support missions which experienced less and
less interference from Syrian ground based air defenses. The
purpose of these raids deep into Syria was to cause strategic
destruction and force the Syrians to redistribute their air
defense assets. This diluted their defenses on the Golan
Heights allowing more freedom of action for IAF ground
support.

    Although the IAF pilots ruled the skies in areas
outside the Syrian air defense network, the Syrian Air Force
kept sending out sorties to stop the Israeli attack. Though
they suffured heavy casualties, they were successful.[73]

    Starting on the thirteenth, faced with stiffening
Syrian ground resistance, intervention of other Arab forces,
and Sinai front priorities, the battle line stabilized.
Israeli air efforts continued to interdict supplies, provided
by the Soviets, as they were being transported to the front.

    The Israelis combined commando raids with BAI as a
means of interdicting Syrian lines of advance. One example
of this occurred on 13 October when an Iraqi division size
unit, moving to the front, was trapped on a road ten
kilometers behind the front lines by Israeli paratroopers.
The Israelis blew up a bridge to the front of the advance and
useing 106mm recoilless rifle fire, hit the rear vehicles
trapping the convoy of the road. With the vehicles unable to
move, the IAF attacked and destroyed the entire convoy.[74]

A second example of an ingenious use of BAI occured during the recapture on Mount Hermon during the last days of the War. Paratroopers were lifted by helicopter with fighter planes covering them while other aircraft conducted a raid on Damascus to further divert the Syrian Air Force. The airmobile operation started at 1400 hours on the twenty-first of October. The Syrians soon discovered that the attempt to recapture Mount Hermon was taking place. They rushed reinforcements to their defensive positions. The IAF anticipated that the Syrian reinforcements would use the road east of Mount Hermon. When the Syrian vehicles started moving along the road to the front, the IAF was waiting for them and destroyed the attempt to reinforce the defenders of Mount Hermon by road. The Syrians responded with fighters and counterattacking airmobile assaults. Again, the IAF anticipated the Syrian plans. The airmobile assault was neutralized when the Israelis destroyed six escorting Syrian fighters and three infantry laden helicopters.[73]

The stablization of the front lines during the last days of the War allowed the Syrians and Iraqis to provide air support for their counterattacks. These attacks were uncoordinated and resulted in Iraqi aircraft attacking Syrian positions and Syrian aircraft mistaking the Jordanians for Israelis. Also, throughout the War, Syrian air defense batteries shot and hit Arab planes numerous times.[74]

Use of Battlefield Air Interdiction

75

On the second day of the War, American military analysts reported that the IAF's two main objectives were to first isolate the Egyptian bridgehead east of the Suez Canal by systematically attacking the bridging equipment to prevent reinforcement of the strong Egyptian force that crossed on the sixth, and by establishing local control of the air over the bridgehead to prevent helicopters or transport aircraft from reinforcing the enemy divisions. The second objective was the liquidation of the Egyptian and Syrian surface-to-air missile sites. The analysts said the role of the SAMs was to shield advancing ground forces against IAF attacks and, "equally important, provide cover for the support forces on the lines of communication."[77]

American analysts recognized that the key to the use of the IAF was in isolating the FEBA from the enemy follow on forces and supplies. These reinforcements and badly needed supplies could be brought into the area by helicopter, transport aircraft, or across the bridges and roads. No matter how they attempted to get to the front, it was the Air Forces job to keep them away. They knew that this would alter the pace of the attack and give Israel time to mobilize and set up a defense. The mission these analysts discribed was battlefield air interdiction.

The Israelis do not use the term battlefield air interdiction. They refer to CAS and interdiction interchangeably when speaking of BAI type missions. They also consider SAM suppression a part of ground support

missions. However, during the War, over 90% of all missions
rated as CAS, were flown at least five kilometers behind the
FEBA and had no positive control measures that are normally
used in CAS missions.[78] The majority of the sorties flown
during the War were actually BAI as described earlier in this
chapter. MG Binyamin Peled, Chief of Staff of the IAF during
the War stated:

> All the other operations of the Air Force
> that were loosely called close support were never
> really close support; they were a combination of
> information put through ground forces channels to
> Air Force planners and decision makers, with the
> autonomous capability of the Air Force to overfly
> the battlefield, find the enemy, report its
> position, ask for an immediate decision and start
> picking them off the ground.[79]

The IAF studied air-to-ground doctrine from World War
II and Vietnam. They reached the conclusion that the
doctrine of air-to-ground operations, laid down by Lord
Tedder in the campaigns of North Africa and the experiences
of the U.S. Air Force, were correct for those times and
circumstances. The 1973 War proved to the IAF that the old
method using CAS did not work and should only be used in an
emergency. They believed that the missile denied the
capability of the pilot to fly over the battlefield, contact
the ground commander, and then try to find and attack the
target. Furthermore, this new threat meant that the pilot
could not be completely dependent on the information provided
by the ground commander. The fact that the ground commander
cannot see much above his normal horizon makes him limited as

a source of information. The pilot needed more than a rough
idea of where the enemy was, the location of friendly troops,
and the topography. He needed a complete lay out of the air
defense systems that would interfere with his bomb run and a
detailed briefing on geographical features he could use to
hide behind prior to the bomb run. This information had to
be given to him by Air Force sources.[40]

These ideas were not new nor isolated to Israel.
United States General William W. Momyer, former Commander of
the Seventh Air Force in southeast Asia, and later Commander
of Tactical Air Command, made the following statement five
months prior to the start of the 1973 War:

> Close air support in another war will be far
> more demanding than what it was in Vietnam and
> probably World War II....Thus, close air support
> will, in all probability, have to be conducted in
> the face of enemy air opposition. In addition, the
> enemy can be expected to have large numbers of
> anti-aircraft weapons and surface-to-air missiles.
> It will be necessary to conduct electronic warfare
> to neutralize the radars that control these
> missiles and to conduct direct air attacks to
> destroy them. Close air support in such a scenario
> is a different way of life than what our forces saw
> in Vietnam.[41]

It must be remembered that the U.S. Air Force did not use the
term battlefield air interdiction during the time of General
Momyer's statement. None the less, it was evident that the
use of ground support was going to have to change.

The Israelis also believed that CAS was a wasted
asset. It supported only a localized situation where the
enemy was already dispersed. It also took too long for the

fighter-bombers to attack each individual target once they
had been deployed.   The results were small gains in small
items.[82]

The IAF concluded that CAS was not the best use of
planes in the ground support role.   MG Peled said, "The place
to get them [the enemy] is where they are concentrated."[83]
The idea was to hit the enemy prior to deployment of their
forces into attack formation.   The destruction of the Iraqi
division, related earlier, was caused by an attack while
moving to the battlefield.   It is an example of how the IAF
decided to use their air-to-ground assets.

The Chief of Staff of the IDF, LTG David Elazar,
agreed with MG Peled that CAS was not used in the classical
way nor would it be used in that role under the same air
defense conditions.   He said:

> I see the Air Force's main role in the support of
> ground forces in interdiction...to achieve
> destruction of the enemy's military infrastructure,
> cause havoc among troop movements and, in one word,
> to paralyze the enemy forces.   Even before 1973, I
> considered the subject of close air support the
> last priority task of the Air Force.   I always
> believed that ground forces, secure from the
> enemy's air activity, should defeat enemy ground
> forces unaided.   The October War reconfirmed my
> belief that close air support is costly in
> casualties, and that there is no positive ratio
> between relatively great losses and limited
> results.[84]

In an interview at the international symposium on
military aspects of the Israeli-Arab conflict, MG Peled gave
three examples of the most important uses of air-to-ground

79

support during the War. All of them were BAI missions.

His first example was the effort needed to keep the major supply and reinforcement route between Gaza and the Suez Canal closed to three enemy brigades. He felt that if the Egyptians could have gotten this route open, they would have started a major offensive in that area. Airpower cut the road needed to resupply and reinforce the offensive. Another example MG Peled gave was the isolation of the Egyptian Third Army from reinforcements or supplies. He believes that all the bridges were destroyed and although four were rebuilt, they could only be used at night. By attacking the roads leading to the Canal, the lodgemont area near the bridges and the bridges themselves, the Air Force helped strangle the Egyptian forces already across. His final example was on the Golan Heights. He believes that airpower should not be measured by the number of tanks that the IAF destroyed but by the fact that the Syrians were turned back along the two main routes through the Golan Heights at 0530 hours on 7 October and did not advance along those routes the rest of the War. Between 0530 hours and 1030 hours, there were no ground forces along those routes. Only the IAF was used to defend them.[55]

There are other reasons, besides the air defense network of the Arabs, that had a major impact on the IAF decision to change the majority of their missions from CAS to BAI. Neither General Elazor nor Feled admitted these reasons publicly. First, unlike the U.S., the Israelis used Army

forward observers to call for and adjust CAS. Prior to the
1973 War, these observers received little realistic training.
The majority of them were reservist. During the
mobilization, for some unexplained reason, many of the
observers went to the wrong locations and did not deploy with
their normal units. It was several days before this
situation was corrected.[84]

Another problem the observers had was trying to talk
to pilots from the ground. The Arabs had a good jamming
ability which caused trouble in adjusting the aircraft and
may have been responsible for IAF planes attacking their own
ground forces.[87]

Finally, there was a problem getting intelligence of
the area to the pilots who were flying into it. TAR flights
were flown but their intelligence was four to six hours old
by the time it was processed. The mobility of the SA6 and
ZSU-23-4s prevented pilots, going to support a unit, from
knowing what defenses they would have to contend with.[88]

Egyptian use of BAI is harder to define because
little information has been printed of the use of the EAF
during the War. It was used primarily during the first day
of the War, during the crossing of the Canal by the IDF in an
attempt to destroy the pontoon bridges as forces moved to
them.[89] Most of the War, the EAF stayed in the rear to
prevent deep interdiction raids. This was due to the
realization that the IAF was far superior in flying ability
and in recognition of a lack of a workable identification

system by the Egyptian air defense network. Several planes
were shot down by their own ground forces. It is estimated
that eighty to ninety percent of the Arab sorties were air
defense sorties over their own territory.[70]

These same problems kept the Syrian Air Forces ground
support to a minimum. They too were successful with their
BAI missions the first few hours of the War. Unlike the EAF,
the Syrians continued to try to support their ground troops.
This effort was soon greatly reduced because of the IAF's
high kill ratio of Syrian planes and the Syrian air defense
system's inability to distinguish friend from foe. Also,
when the IAF started their deep interdiction campaign, the
Syrians kept back planes to protect the home territory. Like
the Egyptians, eighty to ninety percent of Syrian sorties
were dedicated to home defense.[71]

TABLE II

Israeli BAI Sortie Rates

Total number of sorties flown - 11,233.

Sorties for air cover, deep interdiction, air defense - 3,961.

Air-to-ground (CAS and BAI) sorties, Golan - 1,830.

Air-to-ground (CAS and BAI) sorties, Sinai - 5,442

Total air-to-ground sorties - 7,272.

BAI sorties, Golan - 1647.

BAI sorties, Sinai - 4898.

Total BAI sorties - 6545.

Total CAS sorties - 700

Percentage of total sorties flown that were BAI - 58%.

--All numbers are approximately what was flown. Several versions of actual sorties flown have been published.[92]

--Although a total number of AI sorties cannot be found, it is estimated to less than 200. The raids on or near Damascus were the only major AI campaign.

Factors Affecting BAI

Air Defense Systems

The influence of the extensive Arab air defense
network was over emphasized during and shortly after the war.
It was suggested that the air would now be controlled from
the ground. It is true that serious losses were inflicted on
the IAF by the Arab defense system. But, initial estimates
were somewhat exaggerated. In many ways, these air defense
weapons were operated under very favorable conditions. The
heavy Egyptian concentration was deployed prior to
hostilities and under the supervision of Soviet technical
experts and instructors.[93]

It also must be remembered that the initial attacks
by the IAF were not in accordance with doctrine. Because of
the incomplete mobilization, the Air Force was tasked to stop
the advancing forces on two fronts and keep reinforcements
from strengthening enemy positions. To complete this
mission, until ground forces could get to the front, the
doctrine of destroying enemy air defense systems prior to
ground attacks had to be abandoned. Israeli planes attacked
ground targets knowing they were extremely vulnerable.

The IAF also flew against a new weapons system, the
SA6. This mobile launcher, working with the ZSU-23-4
anti-aircraft gun, was unknown to Israeli pilots. But, like
most new weapons systems, there was an antidote to nullify or
at least reduce the effectiveness of this system. When

electronic counter measures (ECM) or flying tactics could not be used, ground forces attacked across the Canal with the mission of destroying the SAM sites.

However, the technological surprise achieved by the Arab forces greatly reduced the effectiveness of the IAF, at least during the early stages of the War. The air defense network challenged the air supremacy that Israel traditionally enjoyed. Not only did they inflict heavy losses, they limited the IAF's airpower the freedom of battlefield air interdiction and almost put a complete halt to close air support. In addition, the IAF required ground forces to aid in the suppression of missile air defenses along the Canal.

In summary, the IAF was denied air supremacy not by Arab air forces but by anti-aircraft ground defenses. However, the Arab success was temporary, indicating that they could be countered one way or another.[74] General Peled argues that the War, rather than demonstrating the superiority of missiles over aircraft, proved that the trend is aircraft over air defense systems.[75]

Electronic Warfare

Electronic countermeasures (ECM) played a major role in the 1973 War. General Hod, former commander of the IAF said, "An ounce of ECM is worth a pound of additional aircraft, in the presence of dense, sophisticated air defense."[76]

A vulnerability of the Arab air defense system was its heavy reliance on electronic radars for early detection, tracking, and targeting of Israeli planes. In many cases, these radars could be neutralized by active ECM. Israel knew what an important force multiplier the control of the electronmagnetic spectrum was. Both sides used extensive and advanced ECM and electronic counter-countermeasures (ECCM). When a radar or communications facility was disrupted or jammed, the air defense and command and control networks became ineffective. Radars, command and control headquarters and electronic sensing devices were the target of interception, interdiction, deception and jamming. The suppression of the Arab air defense network featured the use of direction finding, massive jamming, and radar homing missiles.[97]

In the first few days of the War, the IAF determined that their equipment, used during the War of Attrition, was inadequate in quantity and quality to counter the new Arab systems and tactics. The SA6, SA7, and ZSU-23-4 presented a wider range of frequencies, greater operational capabilities, and previously unsuspecting operational modes. Other problem areas encountered were employment concepts, a lack of knowledge of the threat, poor planning and unfamiliarity with their own countermeasures equipment. Most of the shortcomings were worked out in the first few days of the War. The initial loss rates for the first three days of combat were more than three times those of the remaining days of the conflict.[76]

Israel soon received ECM help from the United States.
This included 200 ECM pods and chaff which consisted of thin
metal strips that were dropped to appear as aircraft on Arab
radar. Advanced U.S. ECMs were able to counter the improved
SA2s and SA3s but American technical experts could not devise
a counter for the SA6 or ZSU-23-4. Most of the SA6s had to
be destroyed by ground artillery fire, by hitting their
antennas, or by being captured by maneuver units.[77]

Command and Control

The command and control of the three forces was
markedly different. This had a definite effect on the use of
airpower by each side.

Israel displayed flexibility and adaptability in
their command structure. The IAF operated in small units
while flying in combat but were organized into large units on
the ground to reduce maintenance and organizational cost. In
order to operate with a large unit that would break into
smaller units, they used a centralized control system that
could delegate authority for a short time to lower echelons
but regain centralized control when needed, according to
changing situations and priorities. This was demonstrated
during the War when the IAF changed major front priorities
from the Sinai on six October, to the Golan Heights from
seven to thirteen October, and back to the Sinai from
fourteen to twenty-four October. This clearly demonstrated
both the flexibility of airpower and the IAF effectiveness in

controlling such transfers. During the War, the changing
tactical situations were quickly accommodated by
reapportioning the sorties to BAI, deep interdiction, SAM
suppression or to what ever was needed to execute the
mission.[100]

The Arab air forces recognized that they were no
match in air-to-air combat with the IAF. They decided to
maintain a defensive posture for the most part. Their
commands emphasized the air defense mission and the need to
keep Israel from flying deep interdiction missions. The air
forces were centrally controlled but had little flexibility
to meet changing requirements. A large number of planes were
sent out on specific missions and were normally unable to
change from the plan. When large casualties occured with
these formations, smaller units of one or two aircraft were
sent out that was an unfamiliar tactic to the pilots.
Several planes were downed because they followed a single
predictable plan no matter what the situation. An example
was such as the attacks on the Israeli bridges near the end
of the War. The formation of separate air defense commands
simplified the command problems, but hampered coordination
with the air defense missile command. Both Syria and Egypt
admit to shooting down some of their own aircraft. The
Syrians shot down several Iraqi planes because of improper
use of the identification, friend or foe (IFF) system. The
Egyptians used the air defense tactic of rapidly switching
the entire air defense network, or selected parts of it, on

and off. This method was used very selectively. The
preferred method of protection from the IAF was the air
defense missile barrier itself. The missile system was
usually left on and EAF pilots had to attempt to fly through
it to return to their oases.[101]

Weapons and Targets

Both air forces used the normal air-to-ground
conventional munitions. There was only limited use of
napalm. The IAF did not strafe in large amounts except for
30mm cannon fire against armor. And the IAF used a limited
number of electro-optical smart munitions. In general, the
IAF used general purpose bombs against interdiction targets,
Cluster Bomb Units (CBUs) were used, when available, against
deployed formations of light armor. Smart munitions or 30mm
cannon were used against armor. The Arabs used mostly
strafing, unguided rockets, and general purpose bombs. The
MIG-17 carries a 37mm cannon and was considered effective
against tracked vehicles.[102]

The electro-optical munitions sent in limited
quantities to the IAF by the U.S. were very effective. The
Maverick TV guided air-to-ground missile was used in the
closing days of the War and was proven successful against
tanks. The Israelis were also resupplied with two
electro-optical glide bombs, the Rockwell International
homing bomb system (HOBOS) and the Martin Marietta Walleye 1
as well as the Northrop target identification system
electro-optical (TISEO).[103]

The effectiveness of the air forces were not as great as expected. This was due in a large part to the inaccuracy inherent in the aircraft as it had to fly low, and fast, and take evasive maneuvers while in the air defense belt.

The IAF claimed to have hit every bridge the Egyptians put across the Canal but this did not stop the flow of troops and supplies. Hundreds of Egyptian sorties were flown against Israeli bridges across the Suez during the final days of the War with the same unsatisfactory results. Neither side could interdict reinforcing troops and supplies by concentrating effort against bridges. There was a high price paid even to get an aircraft to the bridges because numerous air defense systems were usually deployed around it. The accuracy of the ordnance was usually poor because the pilot flew low, fast, and tried to evade anti-aircraft fire. Even if the bridge was hit and damaged, it was usually built in sections which could easily be replaced. Bridges were not an effective BAI target during the War.

Another myth that was illustrated during the War was the use of airpower to kill tanks. There seems to be no scientific evidence to qualify the effectiveness of IAF or Arab airpower in the anti-armor role. Most disabled vehicles, inspected by Israeli ordnance analysts after the War, had received multiple hits so it was not possible to decide what weapons system had made the kill. On the Golan, by accepting heavy casualties in order to play a part in reversing the Syrian armor attack, the IAF certainly had some effect. But, a German tank officer who visited the scene in early November 1973 estimated that eighty percent of Syrian tank losses could be directly attributed to Israeli tank fire where as only twenty percent were destroyed by effects of artillery or air force. This small number of tank losses is compared to the ten to fourteen percent sortie loss rate during the same battle.[104]

Studies of the 1967 War demonstrated that aircraft flying at high speeds and using conventional unguided weapons had limited effect against armor. This lack of effectiveness was greatly increased during the 1973 War when the pilots used unguided general purpose bombs, rockets, and aircraft guns against tanks in an intense anti-air defense environment. It was not until the Arab air defense belt started breaking up and the IAF began using smart munitions that tanks were killed at an acceptable sortie/tank ratio.[105]

Summary

The 1973 Middle East war was primarily a ground action. Israeli airpower did not significantly affect the overall outcome of the land campaigns as it did in 1967.[104] However, the IAF and Arab air forces were heavily committed and, at times, played an important part in specific battles. Because of the extensive integrated Arab air defense system, the IAF did not dominate the battle on the ground as it did during the Six-Day War in 1967.

The reasons for the IAF failure to control the

battlefield as it had six years prior are found in a study of the years between the wars. It started with the Soviet Union increasing support to the Arab countries. The Egyptians first tried to regain their lost territory back during the War of Attrition. When this failed, the Soviets resupplied them, as well as Syria, with the most extensive air defense network outside the Soviet Union. This event changed the balance of airpower in the Middle East. The IAF no longer ruled the skies nor would they be able to give their ground troops the support to which they had become accustomed.

Based on the experience of the Six-Day War and the years leading to the 1973 War, the IAF based its operations plans on the following assumptions:

1. Israel would have at least twenty-four hours notice of an attack.

2. All forces would mobilized and deployed prior to the start of hostilities.

3. Israeli offensive actions would be immediately decisive.

4. Loss of equipment would not be significant and would be comparable to that of the Six-Day War.

5. The "fcg of War" would have minimum affect on Israel because of their pre-war planning.[107]

The first priority of the IAF was to defend Israel, to support the ground forces by keeping Arab planes away from them, and by supporting their maneuver plan with fire support. Israeli fighters, antiaircraft artillery, or missiles contested most Arab air attacks, destroying scores of planes. However, Israeli fighter-bombers were unable to provide effective support for ground units until the Arab air defense network was suppressed.[108]

Israeli aircraft, attacking near the FEBA on both the Sinai and Golan fronts, suffered heavy casualties the first few days. The IAF was forced to abandon their normal tactics of air suppression first, because of the massive attacks by the Arabs. MG Peled said, "Instead of carrying out air defense suppression operations in an orderly manner, we rightly preferred to break them up into small operations and try to do them in the periods in between other things more important at the time."[109]

Losses were heavy and until the mobilization could be completed, the IAF was the only effective military force available. Attacking the Syrian armor, protected by the mobile SA6 and SA7 missiles with the interlocking fires of selfpropelled ZSU-23-4 anti-aircraft guns, proved extremely costly. Approximately thirty-five aircraft were shot down during the afternoon of the sixth.[110]

The major Arab offensive was based on massive attacks of infantry and armor. The primary role of the Arab air forces was to defend their home territory from the IAF. They started the War with a large number of air strikes to slow Israeli reaction to the invasion. Air-to-ground operations were then limited due to the high losses in air-to-air combat with Israeli pilots. The Egyptians made a massive attempt to stop the IDF Canal crossings by bombing the bridges and reinforcements. The Egyptians fought eighteen battles over the bridgehead. In the last week of the War, the Egyptians flew more than 2,500 sorties trying to destroy the bridges and troop concentrations.[111] Again, the IAF destroyed the Egyptian fighter-bombers.

The Arabs generally left defense of their FEBA to their anti-aircraft missile and artillery systems rather than applying fighter cover. Very little information is available on the total sorties flown during the War. Semi-official figures in Arab publications, state that 6,815 Egyptian sorties were flown during the War. The smaller Syrian Air Force and other Arab air forces logged fewer than half the number flown by the Egyptian Air Force. Therefore, it can be estimated that during the War, Arab sorties totaled between 9,000 and 10,000. Approximately half of these were flown for defensive operations while the rest were CAS, BAI, or deep interdiction.[112]

During the War, the IAF fought with its full range of air-to-ground weapons. Most frequently, general purpose bombs were carried by strike aircraft. Cluster bomb units (CBUs) were dropped on SAM sites, convoys, and large area targets. Shrike anti-radiation missiles were frequently fired at SAM radars. Even napalm and unguided rockets were used against ground forces.[113]

Late in the War, the U.S. supplied Israel with a variety of smart munitions including Maverick television camera guided missiles and laser guided bombs. These weapons

proved very effective. Although introduced only in the final

days of the war, the Maverick missile allegedly destroyed

between thirty and fifty Arab vehicles, and bunkers.[114]

The IAF has not officially released any reports on

the strike tactics it evolved while attempting to circumvent

and destroy the intense Arab air defenses. It is known that

Israeli planes attacked SA6 batteries from high angle dives.

They struck other targets inside the Arab defenses at low

level and then popped up to release bombs while evading

SAMs.[115]

The Israeli Air Force achieved major results in four

areas. First, the IAF successfully defended all air space

outside the Arab missile system. Israel claims that only

five Arab air strikes penetrated the Israeli front lines.

Second, they played a major role in stopping the massive

Syrian tank attack that penetrated almost all of the 1967

occupied territory and was nearing the Jordan River. For the

first two days of the War, the IAF was the major effective

force opposing the 1,000 tank Syrian armored thrust. Third,

they defeated the Syrian SAM network protecting the armored

ground forces in a bitter battle that destroyed fifty percent

of the batteries and helped force the remainder to pull back

to fixed positions near Damascus. Finally, a significant

portion of the Syrian war economy was destroyed through deep

interdiction strikes or BAI while supplies were moving to the

front.[116]

Trying to determine losses on either side is a difficult task because of the wide range of estimates. For instance, the IAF claims that only four of their aircraft were shot down in air-to-air combat. But, the commander of an Egyptian MIG-21 fighter regiment told an <u>Aviation</u> <u>Week</u> & <u>Space</u> <u>Technology</u> writer that his three squadrons had accounted for twenty-two gun-camera confirmed air-to-air kills during the War and had the film to prove it.[117]

MG Peled stated that altogether Israel lost 115 aircraft (including helicopters): four fighters in air combat, another one shot down accidentally by an Israeli fighter, ten by accidents or unknown causes, forty-eight by SAMs, and fifty-two by anti-aircraft fire. Peled added that overall, Israel lost one aircraft per one hundred sorties - a figure that compared quite favorable with the loss rate in the 1967 War of four per one hundred sorties.[118]

U.S. intelligence sources estimated that Arab missiles and antiaircraft artillery claimed eighty percent of the Israeli aircraft shot down, air combat ten percent, and ten percent of unknown causes. According to the same sources, 242 Egyptian aircraft, 179 Syrian aircraft, and twenty-one Iraqi aircraft were destroyed by all causes.[119]

While both sides suffered heavy losses, the Soviet Union and later the United States brought in massive amounts of equipment. Soviet transports flew 934 round trips to Egypt and Syria carrying missiles, ammunition, crated aircraft, and other materiel. In addition, an extensive sealift operation supplied an unknown quantity.[120]

U.S. Air Force C-5 and C-141 cargo planes flew 566 round trips to Israel, totaling 22,395 tons. Israeli El Al cargo aircraft carried a further 5,500 tons, and American sealift operation delivered an additional unknown amount. Israel received more than eighty A-4 Skyhawks, forty-eight F-4E Phantoms, a dozen C-130 transports, and a number of helicopters.[121]

Studying how the IDF changed after the War is useful in determining what lessons were learned from it. The pro-Israeli magazine Defence Update commented, "Probably one of the most important lessons the IDF learned from the October war was the unreliability of its air support . The Air Force, aware of its limitations, advocted the acquisition of combat helicopters, especially for tank-killing."[122] During the Lebanon invasion of 1982, the IAF did use helicopters instead of fighter-bombers as the primary air-to-ground tank killer. Military commanders reported a high degree of success using helicopters in an anti-armor role. They reported that sixty percent of the tanks and light armor vehicles were destroyed by helicopter gunships.[123] To compensate for the loss of CAS to the front line troops, the IDF increased their artillery from the end of the 1973 War to the 1982 invasion by 219 percent and made most of it mobile.[124] Although the IAF stayed away from the CAS mission in Lebanon, they learned the usefulness of BAI in 1973 and again used it successfully in 1982. Chaim Herzog report, "The Israeli Air Force was successful in interdiction and in preventing reinforcements from reaching the battlefield, as when a brigade of the Syrian 3rd Armoured Division was caught in a narrow defile and badly mauled."[125] From these statements it can be concluded that the IAF has turned the CAS mission over to the artillery and attack helicopters. Also, they are stressing BAI instead of CAS as the main use of ground support aircraft.

The War changed the way air forces will fly in the future, if faced with the same type of air defense network. No longer will the air force be able to supply close air support in the numbers and accuracy that IDF ground forces expected since the 1967 War and that American troops had available in Vietnam. The Arab air defense network, a lack of intelligence, and poor command and control forced the IAF to fly few CAS missions and use more BAI. It was then that they found that BAI was more effective against ground troops because the pilots were attacking the reinforcements and supplies while moving to the front, before they could disperse. Damage to the enemy was more widespread. The front forces became cut off and could then be handled by the IDF ground forces. Numerous vehicles on both Arab fronts were abandoned because they ran out of gas. The resupply trucks could not get to the front. Battlefield air interdiction was responsible for isolating the first echelons and destroying reinforcements and resupplies.

The main lessons learned about air power in the

ground support role during the 1973 War are now quite

evident.   In a high intensity air defense environment, close

air support is too costly.   Interdicting the enemy prior to

his deployment on the battlefield is the most affective

method of attacking him from the air.   Also, suppression of

the enemy air defense is necessary to have an effective

air-to-ground operation.   The SEAD program is not just an air

force task but must be a joint service obligation.

CHAPTER 4

NOTES

1. Military Studies Department, _Professional Foundations_ (Colo. Springs, CO: USAFA, 1984), P. G-1.

2. Louis Williams, ed., _Military Aspects of the Israeli-Arab Conflict_ (Tel Aviv: University Publishing Projects, 1975), P. 255.

3. FM 100-5, p. 7-11; USAFA, p. G-1.

4. Edgar O'Ballance, _The Third Arab-Israeli War_ (Hamden, CT.: The Shoestring Press, 1972), p. 272.

5. Edgar O'Ballance, "Some Israeli Defence Problems," _The Army Quarterly_, Jan. 1973, P. 152.

6. Stanley M. Ulanoff and David Eshel, _The Fighting Israeli Air Force_ (NY: Arco Publishing Inc., 1985), p. 62.

7. Ulanoff, p. 62.

8. Ulanoff, p. 63.

9. Jimmy H. Church and Robert T. Osterthaler, "The Battle for Air Superiority During the '73 Arab-Israeli War," Paper. USMC Command and Staff College, 1983, p. 34.

10. Committee on Armed Services, _Report of the Special Subcommittee on the Middle East_ (Washington: GPO. 1973), p. 6.
The IAF Commander, MG Feled, said that the EAF lessons from the 1967 War were the need for adequate surveillance systems

to identify incoming aircraft and how effective a counter-air
strike can be on unprotected and non-dispersed aircraft.

11. O'Ballance, "Some Israeli Defence Problems," p.
153.
By May, 1970, at the height of the airwar of the War of
Attrition, only thirty-two Phantoms had arrived in Israel.
F-4s and what was left of the Mirages flew against the
MIG-21s which had the same speed but a much shorter range.

12. Zeev Schiff, "The Israeli Air Force," Air Force
Magazine, Aug. 1976, p 35-36.

13. Edward N. Luttwak and Daniel Horowitz, The Israeli
Army 1948-1973 (Lanham, MD.: University Press of America,
Inc., 1983), P. 302.

14. Ulanoff, pp. 63-64.

15. Ulanoff, p. 69.

16. Ulanoff, pp. 72-73.

17. Edgar O'Blance, No Victor, No Vanquished: The Yom
Kippur War (San Rafael, CA.: Presidio Press, 1978), P. 51.

18. Kohler, p. 35.

19. Lon O. Nordeen, Air Warfare in the Missile Age
(Washington D.C.: Smithsonian Institution Press, 1985), p.
148-150.

20. Ulanoff, pp. 70-73.

21. David Nicolle, "The Holy Day Air War," Air
Enthusiast International May, 1974, p. 240.

22. Nicolle, p. 241.

23. Nicolle, p. 241.

24. Chaim Herzog, The Arab Israeli Wars (New York: Random House, 1982), pp. 285-297.

25. Luttwak, p. 299.

26. Luttwak, pp. 327-336.

27. Amos Perlmatter, Politics and the Military in Israel 1967-1977 (Totowa, N.J.: Frank Cass and Company limited, 1978), pp. 85-87.

28. Jac Weller, "Tanks in the Middle East, Military Review, May 1976, P. 17.

29. D.K. Palit, Return to Sinai (New Delhi: Palit & Palit Publishers, 1974), p. 52-58.

30. Nicolle, p. 252.

31. Zeev Schiff, October Earthquake. Yom Kippur 1973 (Tel Aviv: University Publications Projects Ltd., 1974), p. 260.

32. Williams, p. 240.

33. Historical Evaluations and Research Organization (HERO), "The Arab-Israeli October War, 1973," Combat Data Subscription Service, Vol.2, No.2 Spring 1977, pp. 3-7.

34. Insight Team, The Yom Kippur War, pp. 114-115.

35. Elizabeth Monroe and A.H. Farrar-Hockley, The Arab-Israeli War, October 1973 Background and Events (London: The International Institute for Strategic Studies, 1973), P. 21.

36. The Insight Team of the London Sunday Times, Insight on the Middle East War (London: Times Newspapers Limited, 1974), pp. 56-57.

37. Insight Team, <u>Insight</u>, p. 57.

38. Kenneth S. Brower, "The Yom Kippur War," <u>Military Review</u>, March 1974, pp. 25-31; K. Subrabmanyam, "The Lessons of the 1973 Arab-Israeli War," <u>The Institute for Defence Studies and Analysis Journal</u>, Vol.VI, No.2, January 1974, pp. 428-442.

39. Chaim Herzog, <u>The War of Atonement</u> (Boston: Little, Brown and Company, 1975), pp. 257-258.

40. Nicolle, pp. 242-243.

41. Avraham Adan, <u>On the Banks of the Suez</u> (Jerusalem: Edanim Publications, 1979), p. 81.

42. Williams, pp. 240-241.

43. Schiff, <u>October Earthquake</u> p. 60.

44. Schiff, <u>October Earthquake</u> pp. 69-73.

45. Personal interview with COL. Doron Kadmiel, Israeli Defense Force, 10 Jan. 1986.

46. O'Balance, <u>No Victor, No Vanquished</u>, p. 290.

47. Ulanoff, p. 91.

48. Nicolle, p. 242.

49. Ulanoff, p. 91.

50. Schiff, <u>October Earthquake</u>, p. 78.

51. Schiff, <u>October Earthquake</u>, pp. 80 and 113.

52. Herzog, <u>War of Atonement</u>, pp. 173,175,179.

53. Ulanoff, p. 93.

54. Schiff, <u>October Earthquake</u>, p. 114.

55. Adan, pp. 119 and 160.

56. Adan, pp. 172 and 188; O'Ballance, <u>No Victor, No</u>

Vanquished, p. 134.

57. Adan, p. 225.

58. Herzog, War of Atonement, p. 206; Schiff, October Earthquake, p. 213.

59. Ulanoff, p. 103.

60. Schiff, October Earthquake, p. 213.

61. O'Ballance, No Victor, No Vanquished, p. 233; Schiff, October Earthquake, p. 247.

62. Insight Team, Yom Kippur, p. 343.

63. Ulanoff, p. 109.

64. Nicolle, p. 246-247.

65. Nicolle, p.247; Ulanoff, p. 109.

66. Schiff, October Earthquake, pp. 254-269; Ulanoff, pp. 109-115.

67. T.N. Dupuy, Elusive Victory (New York: Harper and Row Publishers, 1978), p. 450; C.E. Olschner, "The Air Superiority Battle in the Middle East, 1967-1973," Thesis USACGSC, 1978, p. 46.

68. Allen, p. 82; Herzog, War of Atonement, p. 87; Insight Team, Yom Kippur, p. 161; Schiff, October Earthquake, p. 66.

69. Dupuy, Elusive Victory, p. 450.

70. Herzog, War of Atonement, p. 125; Schiff, October Earthquake, p. 152-153.

71. Ulanoff, pp. 96-98.

72. Schiff, October Earthquake, p. 167; Ulanoff, p. 99.

73. Martin L. Musella, "Air Operations During the 1973

Arab-Israeli War and the Implications for Marine Aviation,"

USMC Command and Staff College, 1985, p. 31.

74. U.S. Army Command and General Staff College

(UASACGSC), RB 100-2, Vol. 1, The 1973 Middle East War (Ft.

Leavenworth: CGSC, 1976), p. 5-9.

75. Herzog, War of Atonement, p. 143; USACGSC, RB100-2,

p.5-10.

76. Nicolle, p. 252.

77. Drew Middleton, "Israelis Two Objectives," The New

York Times, 8 Oct. 1973, p. 8, Col. 7.

78. Nicolle, p. 252; Williams, pp. 255-256.

79. Williams, p. 255.

80. Williams, p. 256.

81. Bernard Kornhauser and B.J. de Florio, "Value of

Close Air Support," Report, Arlington, VA., 30 June 1976, p.

133.

82. Jeffery Greenhut, "International Symposium on the

Military Aspects of the Arab-Israeli Conflict, Jerusalem,

12-17 October 1975," Aerospace Historian Vol. 23, No. 1,

March, 1976, p. 22.

83. Greenhut, p. 22.

84. Williams, p. 249.

85. Williams, pp. 241-242.

86. Martin van Creveld, "Military Lessons of the Yom

Kippur War: Historical Perspectives," Report. The Center for

Strategic and International Studies, 1975, P. 37.

87. TRADOC, "Lessons Learned from the 1973 Middle East

Crisis," Report. 11 Jan. 1974, p. 23.

88. Weapons Systems Evaluation Group, "The October 1973 Middle East War (U) Vol. IV: Air Operations," Report. May 1975, P. 17. SECRET. Several portions of this report are unclassified.

89. Williams, pp. 242-243.

90. Williams, p. 242.

91. Williams, p. 242.

92. HERO, "Comparative Analysis, Arab and Israeli Combat Performance 1967 and 1973 Wars," Report. 1977, pp. 25-32.

93. C.N. Barclay, "Lessons from the October War," Army, March 1974, p. 26.

94. Hans F. Raser, "Defense Suppression," Air University Review, July-August 1978, pp. 28-29.

95. Bonner Day, "New Role for the Israeli Air Force," Air Force, Aug. 1978, p. 37.

96. O'Ballance, No Victor, No Vanquished, p. 306.

97. Military Studies Department, Airpower in Warfare (Colo. Springs, CO.: USAFA, 1983), pp. 22-23.

98. Richard V. Hartman and Julian S. Lake, "Air Electronic Warfare," Proceedings, Oct. 1976, p. 47-48.

99. O'Ballance, No Victor, No Vanquished, p. 303.

100. Williams, p. 244.

101. Musella, p. 69-70.

102. USACGSC, RB 100-2, p. 5-13.

103. Barry Miller, "U.S. Equips Israel With 'Smart'

Guided Weapons," <u>Aviation Week & Space Technology</u>, 5 Nov. 1973, p. 48.

104.   Sandia National Laboritories, "A Historical Analysis of the Effectiveness of Tactical Air Operations Against and in Support of Armored Forces," October 1980, pp. 105-106.

105.   Kornhauser, p. 125.

106.   HERO, Comparative Analysis, Arab and Israeli combat Performance 1967 and 1973 Wars," Report, 1977, p. 5.

107.   Greenhut, p. 22.

108.   Nordeen, p. 162.

109.   Schiff, "The Israeli Air Force," p. 37.

110.   Frank Aker, <u>October 1973:   The Arab-Israeli War</u> (Hamden, CT.:   Archon Books, 1985), P. 50.

111.   Dupuy, <u>Elusive Victory</u>, p. 550.

112.   USACGSC, RB 100-2, p. 5-13.

113.   USACGSC, RB 100-2, p. 5-13.

114.   USACGSC, RB 100-2, p. 5-13.

115.   Nordeen, p.167.

116.   Herbert J. Coleman, "Israeli Air Force Decisive in War," <u>Aviation Week & Space Technology</u>, 3 Dec. 1973, p. 18.

117.   "Egypt Makes Major Military Shifts," <u>Aviation Week & Space Technology</u>, Dec. 17, 1973, p. 18.

118.   Nordeen, p. 163.

119.   Nicolle, p. 248.

120.   Nicolle, p. 252.

121.   Nicolle, p. 252.

122. David Eshel, "Modern Inter-Arms Concepts," <u>Defence</u> <u>Update</u> <u>International</u>, No. 69, 1985, p. 35.

123. Richard A. Gabriel, <u>Operation</u> <u>Peace</u> <u>for</u> <u>Galilee</u>, (New York: Hill and Wang, 1984), p. 212.

124. Gabriel, p. 21.

125. Herzog, <u>The</u> <u>Arab-Israeli</u> <u>Wars</u>, p. 400.

CHAPTER 5

CONCLUSIONS

Before drawing conclusions about the affects of the battlefield air interdiction campaign of the 1973 Middle East War, several other matters should be addressed. The historical lessons are more valuable if they can be interpreted in a contemporary setting. Therefore, this chapter includes the following:

1. The differences between the Middle East theater and that of NATO. These differences are contrasts of:

    a. Terrain

    b. Human habitation

    c. Weather

    d. Distance

    e. Arab and Soviet tactics.

2. The changes in technology which have occured since 1973 and the implications of these new systems on the airwar.

3. Conclusions made from the study in relation to the future use of the air-to-ground mission.

The NATO Environment

A comparison of Central Europe to the Middle East is necessary because the differences between the theaters impact

on the BAI mission. Geographically, the rolling hills,
trees, fog and dwellings in Central Europe combine to greatly
reduce the range at which tanks and similar vehicles can be
acquired by pilots. The vehicles can easily blend into the
countryside. Of course, the terrain features also serve to
channel the threat forces, making routes of advance somewhat
more predictable and deployment into battle formation harder.
Terrain features also serve to impede lateral movement across
the battlefield as well as to cause greater reliance to be
placed upon existing road and rail networks. In contrast to
the broad open Sinai, much of European terrain dictates less
ground maneuver and closer engagement ranges than those of
the 1973 War. A pilot will have a harder time acquiring a
target and less time to aim or direct a shot because of the
vegetation and hills. But target planners will have an
easier time establishing where and when specific threat units
will be. BAI targets will be easier to attack because the
second echelon threat will stay on the roads and, if
attacked, may have a harder time deploying due to the terrain
and urbanization. If the enemy is already deployed into an
attack formation, the pilot will have a harder time finding
the target.[1]

The manmade obstacles and urbanization are another
terrain difference. There is greater opportunity for the BAI
pilot to slow the enemy by attacking the numerous choke
points in the villages of Europe. The road network is much
more established throughout Europe but there are many more

bridges and tunnels that have been built through, over, or around water obstacles and mountains. Although it was evident from the 1973 War that bridges are not good targets to attack, they can be attacked prior to the enemy getting to them. Also, because of the numerous obstacles, a very significant portion of the enemy's transportation resources will be needed to carry bridging equipment.

Flying time to the FEBA is another important difference between the IAF's environment and that of NATO forces. In most cases, the Israelis were only a few minutes flying time from the front. They were able to carry more ordnance and loiter longer than NATO pilots can. The IAF also had shorter turn around times and were closer to maintenance facilities. Some NATO missions originate from England. Although forward basing is used, higher level maintenance for many aircraft is still done in England.[2]

Another major difference between the Middle East and Europe is the flying weather. During the 1973 War, weather was not a factor in reducing flying time. This is not the case in Europe. When asked about European weather, General Charles A. Gabriel, U.S. Air Forces in Europe and Commander, Allied Air Forces Central Europe stated that due to the ceiling and visibility during eighty percent of the winter, the only plane that can do a credible job is the F-111.[3]

Not only will the weather ground many aircraft, the low ceiling and haze will affect standoff weapons such as the Maverick. Weather needed for an Imaging-Infrared (IIR)

Maverick (AGM-65D) to obtain target detection at six kilometers, five degrees elevation and launch at four kilometers is only present about fifty-five percent of the time during the winter months.[4]

Comparing Arab and Soviet Forces

The capabilities displayed by the Arab countries in the 1973 War did not necessarily reflect the Soviet strengths and weaknesses at that time. The Arabs received a tremendous amount of new equipment between 1967 and 1973. The Arabs' lack of technical sophistication and language problems both with instructors and in manuals, limited the proficiency of the operators. In addition, neither the equipment nor the employment of assets were representative of what the Soviets could do. Therefore, it is incorrect to make the assumption that the airwar of 1973 was strictly comparable to a U.S.-Soviet conflict.

The Soviets declined to provide the Arab air forces with the newest Soviet aircraft. Had they provided the newest generation of fighter bombers the Egyptians might have been more effective in their attempt to stop the IDF from crossing the Canal. Also, because the Arabs did not have a significant medium bomber threat, the IAF could use a larger portion of their sorties for offensive air support rather than keeping a sizable force back for air defense of their cities.

Although the Arab emphasis on SAM's and anti-aircraft guns does reflect a strong Russian influence, both the equipment and employment of the Arabs differed significantly from that of the Soviets. The Arab countries were not provided the full range of complementary SAM systems which makes the Soviet air defense system so hard to penetrate. If the Arabs had had operational long range high altitude SA4s, their SA3s and SA6s would have been less vulnerable to attack. Besides the range, the Arabs lacked the density of assets which makes the Soviet defense so formidable. The lack of density of SAM's on the Sinai front enabled the Israelis to ultimately achieve air superiority over the Egyptian Third Army. Conversely, the Israelis never gained a high degree of air superiority over the Golan Heights where the density of SAM's was higher for much of the War.

The limitations on equipment was compounded by the Arabs refusal to totally employ Soviet doctrine. The SA6 and ZSU-23-4 are highly mobile systems that were developed to stay as close to the FEBA as possible. Their mobility makes them well suited for offensive operations because they can keep up with mechanized and armor forces. The Egyptians, however, did not aggressively echelon these weapons across the Canal after the units had established defensive positions. Because of this, the systems were not utilized to their full potential in the Sinai. Egyptian attacks did not have the air defense support needed and were defeated when ever they ventured out of the protective air defense umbrella.

In conclusion, although the Arab countries used Soviet equipment and were trained by Russians, it would not be accurate to believe that their performance was a good indication of Soviet capabilities in 1973. Flying against the Arabs was probably the best trained and most experience air force in the world. It was certainly equipped with more sophisticated and modern technical equipment than its enemy.

Technical Changes

There have been many changes to the East-West weapons systems that were used during the 1973 War. As better aircraft have been developed, so have better surface-to-air missiles, as well as ECMs to jam the SAMs. Other developments also have had a considerable impact on the conduct of air operations.

Three developments would seem to have the potential to bring dramatic changes to the conduct of air warfare. These are the use of airborne early warning and control systems, drones, and stand-off weapons.

The use of airborne early warning and control systems has emerged since the 1973 War. They are highly sophisticated airborne platforms with extensive radar and electronic equipment. They can look over the horizon to identify targets and direct friendly forces to intercept them. The U.S. Air Force's version known as the Airborne Warning and Control System (AWACS) is in an E-3A aircraft which is air refuelable. The Navy has its own version to detect not only aircraft but also ships and submarines.

These systems are used to control friendly assets by identifying targets and directing their destruction. The airborne system can also be used with ground air defense units. The U.S. will be fielding the Adaptable Surface Interface Terminal (ASIT) which will allow direct link between AWACS and an air defense battalion.* This system is a major force multiplier because of its ability to look out beyond ground radars, track multiple targets at the same time, determine target data, and direct aircraft or SAMs to interdict the threat.

Drones and remotely piloted vehicles (RPVs) are pilotless aircraft used for reconnaissance, target acquisition, deception, and targeting. A drone flies a preprogrammed course, sometimes with onboard navigation equipment for correction of inflight deviations. The RPV is controlled from the ground using radio or onboard television cameras. RPVs can be jammed but drones cannot. The advantages of these types of aircraft is obvious. They cost less than a plane, are almost impossible to shoot down, and pilots are not wasted.

The primary mission of drones is reconnaissance. The electronic sensors on board are light and reusable. The drone flys slow and low, and because of its size, it is hard to detect even on radar.

Target acquisition is another mission for the pilotless aircraft. The artillery can have direct link with the RPV to give instant target identification. The U.S. RPV was first tested with the artillery as the main proponet. Due to the lengthy loiter time, the RPV can stay over the battlefield to give corrections to air or ground units attacking a target and then give bomb damage assessment (BDA).

Drones and RPVs also have combat roles. They can carry electronic gear to simulate a larger aircraft or groups of aircraft. Acting as decoys, they can spearhead strike missions by detecting enemy radar and allowing piloted aircraft using antiradiation missiles to attack enemy air defense systems.[7]

The U.S. RPV flys with a laser device for targeting. Its TV picture is transmitted to the controller who can find a target and mark it with a laser. The target is then attacked with an artillery round or air-to-ground missile which uses the laser to home in on the target. A secondary mission for RPVs is to identify and mark a target for destruction. An example is using it to find and mark a target while another aircraft fires a precision missile and leaves the area before being detected or within range of air defense weapons.

There is little distinction between powered air-to-surface missiles and electro-optically controlled bombs and glide bombs which rely on kinetic energy to reach the target once released. Guidance systems include radio and wire command guidance, laser homing and various optical applications such as TV and imaging infrared. These

munitions allow the pilot to attack a target from a distance
without having to fly over it.

Another advantage is that one precision munition from
one sortie can destroy a target that many sorties would have
to attack with conventional munitions. Precision guided
munitions, although used in Vietnam and at the end of the
1973 War by the IAF, did not have great impact due to their
limited employment. If the IAF had had access to air
delivered precision guided munitions at the start of the War,
they could have hit the bridges without taking heavy
casualties. The same case can be made with the extremely
high loss rate suffered by the Egyptians when they tried to
destroy the Israeli bridges at the end of the War with
conventional munitions.

The most prolific of the precision weapons is the
Maverick. It possesses a range of guidance techniques and a
hard target or a blast fragmentation warhead. Initially, the
Maverick was developed using a TV guidance system. There are
now 19,000 of this model, the AGM-65A, in the USAF inventory.
The "B" model has significant scene magnification allowing a
longer range of small targets. There are approximately
7,000AGM-65Bs in the inventory. The AGM-65C uses a laser
system. An air or ground laser marks the target for the
missile to home in on. This is good in a close support role
to kill tanks now that the Army ground observers have laser
designators. The AGM-65D is imaging infrared controlled and
can function in darkness or smoke against camouflaged

targets.

There are some problems with precision munitions.
All but the very latest and most advanced have a hard time
finding a target during times of limited visibility. They
can lock on to a different target than the one selected by
the pilot, for example, a burning vehicle near the designated
target.°

The Bekaa Valley

The 1982 Israeli invasion of southern Lebanon,
Operation "Peace for Galilee," has been portrayed by many
analysts as evidence of the complete domination of the new
air weapons systems over air defense. Indeed the IAF used
the new systems to their full advantage.

On June 9, the IDF attacked north against Palastine
Liberation Organization (PLO) and Syrian positions. The
invasion itself started on 6 June. At 1400 hours, The IAF,
working in concert with the field artillery, attacked the
Syrian defense system in the Bekaa Valley. The Syrian
defenses were formidable. They included fifteen SA6, two
SA3, and two SA2 missile batteries with some 2⁰ missiles
ready to launch and supporting anti-aircraft guns. These
were concentrated in the valley and along the Syrian
border.⁹ The IAF had been working on a plan to destroy the
Syrian air defenses since the end of the 1973 War. The plan
successfully incorporated the use of the newest technical
equipment available.

Using artillery, surface-to-surface missiles, EW

jamming and deception, the IAF was able to knock out ten of the nineteen SAM batteries within the first ten minutes of their first air attack. Before the attack was over, the IAF claims to have destroyed seventeen batteries and damaged two others without losing an aircraft.[10]

The Syrians counter-attacked by sending up sixty MIG-21 and MIG-23 fighters to drive the IAF off. But, the Israelis had stripped away the ground control devices used by the Syrian pilots and had an airborne early warning plane to vector them to attack headings to intercept the Syrians. In other words, the Syrians were flying blind while the IAF was aware of where the Syrians were and the best way to attack them. In one of the largest dogfights since World War II, the Syrians lost twenty-nine aircraft while the IAF says it did not lose a single plane.[11]

The Syrians rushed in additional missile batteries into Lebanon to reconstitute an effective air defense umbrella. The IAF destroyed them as fast as they were deployed and swept Syrian interceptors from the air. By 12 June, Syria had lost eighty planes in air combat without an Israeli loss. The IAF did lose one plane to ground fire.[12] According to U.S. sources, a total of twenty-three SAM batteries were destroyed.[13]

There are two major reasons for the success of the IAF. First, the Israelis were able to change their tactics to take advantage of the new weapons systems and command and control devices. Second, the Syrians were inefficient. The

Israelis used RPV's for over a year to gain reconnaissance
information on the Syrian SAM batteries. They knew the
location of every site. The tactics employed to destroy the
Syrian air defense system were much like those used by the
U.S. Air Force in Vietnam but with innovations. Jamming and
deception were extensive using RPV's, drones, and manned
aircraft. The unmanned aircraft were able to get the Syrians
to turn on their radars which opened them up for jamming or
destruction by anti-radiation missiles. While this was
happening, artillery was destroying any batteries within
range. The aircraft flying SAM suppression flew against a
diluted network and knew the location of each battery that it
was to destroy.[14]

The majority of the blame for the destruction on the
Syrian air defense system has to lie with the Syrians
themselves. They did not employ Soviet air defense tactics.
Once positioned in the Bekaa Valley, most of the batteries
failed to move again or dig in to improve their chances of
survivability. Also, many radars were activated to track the
unmanned aircraft that the Israelis flew at them. This gave
away their position and frequency. The lack of dummy
emitters and decoy SAM batteries reduced radar longevity.[15]

The Battle of the Bekaa Valley is important to the
use of battlefield air interdiction for several reasons.
First, it shows the capabilities of systems that have become
available since the 1973 War. It demonstrates how air
defense networks can be overcome to allow for air-to-ground

support missions. Finally, it shows the importance of
tactics keeping pace with technology. However, too much
emphasis is sometimes placed on this battle. Although the
IAF totally destroyed the Syrian Air Force and air defense
system, it must be remembered that the major reasons for
their defeat were errors made by the Syrians themselves and
not just the superiority of the new technology used by the
IAF. The Soviets will probably not make the same mistakes as
the Syrians.

Conclusions

The most startling aspect of the 1973 War was the
curtailment of Israeli air supremacy. In 1967, the roads
were cluttered with burned out Arab vehicles that had been
attacked by the IAF. After 1967, Israel thought their
airpower would continue to make up for a lack of manpower and
weapons systems. Their Air Force received the vast majority
of defense funding and other support. The Israeli General
Staff failed to plan for the contingency of not having
control of the skys and not being able to use their "flying
artillery" to stop ground attacks.

However, the Egyptians and, to a lesser degree, the
Syrians, learned a lot from the 1967 War. They planned to
correct their weaknesses, limit Israeli strengths, and take
advantage of Israeli shortcomings. The Arab's pre-1973 years
were a time of planning new strategy and tactics, testing
them during the War of Attrition, and then refining their
plans and re-arming themselves for the 1973 War.

When the 1973 War started, the IAF had, in order, three main missions: the air defense of Israeli territory and the battlefield, interdiction of the enemy supply, reinforcement, and transportation system in order to paralyze his forces, and close air support of the ground forces.[16] The IAF was successful in its first mission of air defense. Arab aircraft and missiles did not have an impact on the mobilization, deployment, or ground operations of the IDF. Arab planes were unable to penetrate into Israeli airspace. Israeli aircraft were also able to interdict the Arab forces, destroying an Iraqi division before it engaged Israeli ground forces. In Egypt, where approximately a hundred SAM sites were deployed in rear areas and another sixty batteries were deployed near the Canal, Israeli aircraft penetrated and attacked targets of importance. This had the effect of forcing the Arab air forces to allot eighty to ninety percent of their sorties to air defense. But, even when these successes are accepted, no question exists that the Arab air defense system succeeded in certain cases in neutralizing one of the better air forces in the world.

The Arab air defense system was the most extensive in the world outside of the Soviet Union. The Arabs knew that this system had to be able to deny the IAF the airspace over the Arab maneuver forces. Without it the Arab forces would be destroyed from the air as they had been in 1967. The system was a complex network of fully integrated SA2, SA3, and SA6, missiles along with the ZSU-23-4 anti-aircraft gun.

The shoulder fired SA7, also sometimes mounted on a vehicle, was also used. The Arabs knew their pilots and planes were not a match for the Israelis so they were kept to the rear for air defense. If airpower was taken from Israel, the Arabs believed their ground units could defeat the IDF or at least win a large enough victory to gain a political settlement that would return their lost territory to them.

The use of SAMs by the enemy seriously affected the IAF's mission in at least two ways. First, it forced the diversion of aircraft into suppression missions so that they were not available for other activities. This did not change Israeli doctrine, which still gives the Air Force an initial role against air defenses, including missiles. The Israelis felt that a main objective of the Air Force is to destroy as many enemy ground forces as it can. It must be able to act independently against the air defenses of enemy ground units. Although they accept that their own ground forces can act in support of aircraft by placing artillery against enemy missile batteries, the need for the Air Force to act quickly and in places out of range of the weapons of Israeli ground units, makes it impossible for the Air Force to give up the suppression mission.

A second way in which the Arab air defense network affected the Air Force's mission was to make ground support more difficult and CAS almost impossible. This, of course, was a big change from the 1967 War. In ideal conditions of no enemy opposition and complete freedom to overfly and reconnoiter the battlefield almost completely safe from meaningful air defense systems, the IAF was a very important weapons system.

Since the 1973 War, the Israelis object to the old procedures of close air support for the following reasons. First, CAS is no longer possible because the introduction of the missile now prohibits the pilot from loitering over the battlefield to acquaint himself with the terrain and the flow of battle before launching an attack. The IAF has concluded that CAS is not the best way of using airpower because with the enemy already dispersed, it is difficult for the Air Force to select and attack targets. The time to attack the enemy is when he is concentrated, before he has deployed. The Iraqi division was destroyed while moving to the battle, not on the FEBA. Also, CAS is costly and often there is no positive correlation between great losses and results. Finally, ground force, if secure from enemy air activity, should be able to defeat enemy forces unaided. Nonetheless, in spite of these arguments, both Israeli ground and air commanders agree that some situations will demand close air support.

The air defense missile has also changed the nature of intelligence required by the Air Force. Intelligence must be far more detailed and topographical, concerned with things like lines of sight for missile defenses. The ground commander, who cannot see above the horizon, and is too busy with his own problems, cannot supply this type of

124

information. Therefore, the IAF believes that the format,
speed, and clarity of their information about the situation
on the ground, particularly in the combat zone, should be the
responsibility of the Air Force.[17]

Another lesson that the IAF has drawn from the War is
the need to restructure its command and control system.
Because the IAF cannot afford the quantity of aircraft that
would permit the establishment of separate commands for each
type of mission, it needs a command and control system that
permits centralized control, delegation of that control for
short periods, and the reestablishment of central control,
when needed. Only in this way can they use the same aircraft
in different roles.[18]

The new technology developed since the War would
appear to have profound effect on the airwar. Especially if
only the Bekaa Valley is examined. But countermeasures and
counter-tactics are also being developed. Bekaa Valley was a
great IAF success but so was the pre-emptive strike of 1967.
The stand-off weapon, such as the Maverick, will mean that
fewer sorties will be needed to destroy a point target but it
is still limited by range of the system and its control
device. Also, there are anti-aircraft missiles that can fire
out to the range of the aircraft thus nullifying part of its
advantage. Other problem areas or counter-devices will
effect the performance of the technology developed since the
War that was mentioned earlier in this chapter.

The success of the Arab air defense umbrella is

interpreted by many to demonstrate that air superiority will no longer have a significant effect on the ground support battle. It is argued that given more time, electronic countermeasures would have reduced the effectiveness of the SAM's. But countermeasures lead to counter-countermeasures and it is impossible to predict if attack or defense is likely to be more successful. It should be remembered that the reason the air defense umbrella was not fully effective against the IAF operating over the west bank of the Canal was that Israeli ground forces had neutralized many of the SAM batteries.

The future of the combat aircraft is still unsettled. But from the 1973 War, it is obvious that although it still is a powerful weapons system, it is no longer supreme in a sophisticated air defense environment. For that reason, the U.S. Air Force's doctrine and the Army's expectations for close air support could result in a costly waste of resources. It was proven in the 1973 War that battlefield air interdiction was less costly and more effective to the overall defense plan of Israel.

Based on this study, it can be concluded that:

1. Close air support is not the best use of air assets in a high density air defense environment.

2. Battlefield air interdiction is more effective to the operational ground commander than close air support.

3. Localized control of air defense systems is needed to allow the use of air-to-ground assets.

4. Suppression of enemy air defense systems is a joint service responsibility.

Areas for Further Study

This study has raised additional issues and areas that lend themselves to additional in depth research.

Suggested topics are as follows:

1. The most effective command and control system needed to exercise the ground support mission.

2. The establishment of a joint element at corps and higher headquarters whose sole mission is joint attack of enemy air defense.

3. A priority classification system for BAI targets.

4. The use of Army forward air controllers.

CHAPTER 5

NOTES

1. P.A. Erickson, "The '73 War: Implications for U.S. Army Forces in NATO," Thesis. USACGSC, 1978, p. 128.

2. Michael Skinner, USAFE - A Primer of Modern Air Combat in Europe (Novato, CA.: Presido Press, 1983), p. 35.

3. Benjamin F. Schemmer. "We Can Count On Our Allies. I'm Not Sure the Warsaw Pact Can Count On Theirs," Armed Forces Journal, January 1982, pp. 69-70.

4. Ed L. Battle and John r. Shea, Sensor Improvement for Aircraft Performing the Night/Adverse Weather Battlefield Interdiction Mission (Arlington, VA.: Institute for Defense Analysis, Evaluation Division, June 1980) p.20.

5. Musella, PF. 66-70.

6. Richard L. McCabe, "Middle East Challenges ADA Defense Design," Air Defense Artillery, Summer 1985, p. 29.

7. James F. Dunnigan, How to Make War (New York: William Morrow and Company, Inc., 1982), pp. 106-107.

8. Cambell, p. 40.

9. Charles E. Mayo, "Lebanon: An Air Defense Analysis," Air Defense Artillery, Winter, 1983. p. 22.

10. Mayo, p. 22.

11. "A Terrible Swift Sword," <u>Newsweek</u>, 21 June 1982, p. 24.

12. Herzog, <u>The Arab-Israeli Wars</u>, p. 389.

13. Nordeen, p. 183.

14. Nordeen, p. 184.

15. Nordeen, p. 184.

16. Greenhut, p. 249.

17. Greenhut, p. 252.

18. Greenhut, p. 252.

APPENDICES

APPENDIX 1

ABBREVIATIONS

ACC   Air Component Commander
ADA   Air Defense Artillery
AI   Air Interdiction
AWACS   Airborne Warning and Control System
BAI   Battlefield Air Interdiction
BCE   Battlefield Coordination Element
CAS   Close Air Support
EAF   Egyptian Air Force
EW   Electronic Warfare
FLOT   Forward Line of Own Troops
FSCL   Fire Support Coordination Line
IAF   Israeli Air Force
IDF   Israeli Defense Force
JFC   Joint Force Commander
LCC   Land Component Commander
SAF   Syrian Air Force
SAM   Surface-to-air Missile
SEAD   Suppression of Enemy Air Defenses
TAR   Tactical Air Reconnaissance
USACGSC   U.S. Army Command and General Staff
                 College

APPENDIX 2

DEFINITION OF TERMS

1. Air Interdiction--Air operations conducted to destroy, neutralize, or delay the enemy's military potential before it can be brought to bear effectively against friendly forces, at such distance from friendly forces that detailed integration of each air mission with the fire and movement of friendly forces is not required.

2. Allocation--The translation by the tactical air control center of the apportionment decision into total numbers of sorties by aircraft type available for each operation or task.

3. Apportionment--The determination and assignment of the total expected effort by percentage and/or geographic areas for a given period of time.

4. Battlefield Air Inderdiction(BAI)--Air action against hostile surface targets which are in a position to directly affect friendly forces and which requires joint planning and coordination. While BAI requires coordination in joint planning, continuous coordination may not be required during the execution stage.

5. Battlefield Coordination Element(BCE)--A land component

commander liaison element which is collocated with the
requests for tactical air support, monitors and interprets
the land battle situation for the TACC, and provides the
necessary interface for the exchange of current intelligence
and operational data.

6.   Close Air Support(CAS)--Air support of surface operations
by attacking hostile targets in close proximity to friendly
surface forces and that requires detailed integration of each
air mission with the fire and movement of those forces.

7.   Counter Air--Air operations conducted to attain and
maintain a desired degree of air superiority by the
destruction or neutralization of enemy forces.

8.   Forward Edge of the Battlefield(FEBA)--The forward limit
of the main battle area(MBA).

9.   Fire Support Coordination Line(FSCL)--A line established
by a ground commander to facilitate the rapid execution of
fires by surface to surface or to air to surface means. It
is usually well forward of the FEBA.

10.   Forward Line of Own Troops (FLOT)--A line which
indicates the most forward positions of friendly forces in
any kind of military operation at a specific time.

11.   Second Echelon--Enemy ground military formations not
directly engaged in the battle at the FLOT and positioned
behind the forces in contact as a reserve force, a
Soviet-style second echelon, an operational maneuver group,
or a follow-on force.

12.   Sortie--One aircraft making one takeoff and one landing.

An operational flight by one aircraft.

13. Suppression of Enemy Air Defenses(SEAD)--That activity that neutralizes, destroys, or temporarily degrades enemy air defense systems in specific area by physical attack and/or electronic warfare to enable tactical air operations to be successfully conducted.

14. Tactical Air Control Center(TACC)--The principle air operations installation from which all aircraft and air warning functions of tactical air operations are controlled.

Source: FM 101-5-1, Operational Terms and Symbols (Final Draft), 1985.

APPENDIX 3

·MAPS

Source: Department of History, Selected Readings in Warfare Since 1945, West Point, N.Y.:   USMA, 1981.

MAP I – Sinai, 6-13 October 1973

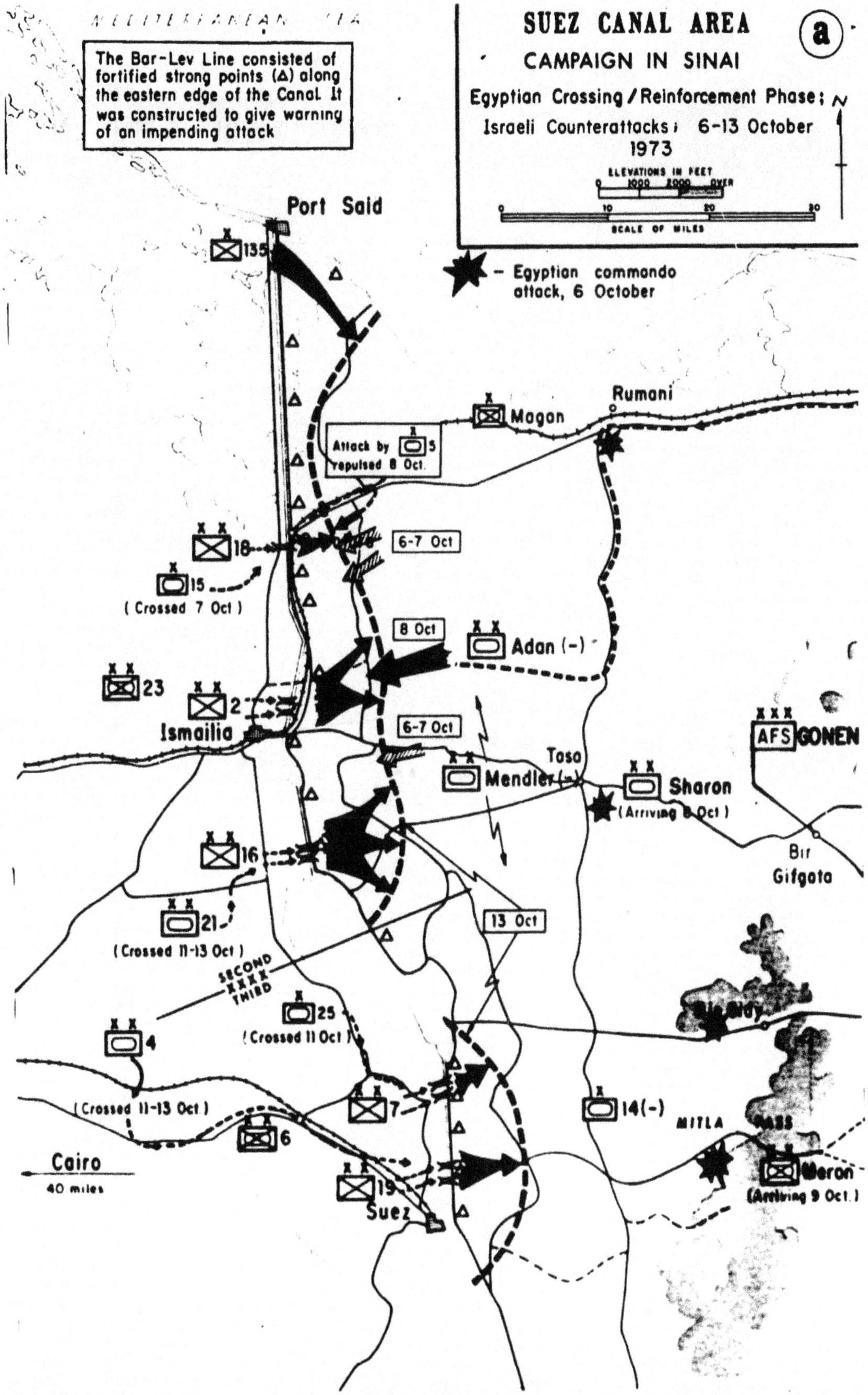

The Bar-Lev Line consisted of
fortified strong points (Δ) along
the eastern edge of the Canal. It
was constructed to give warning
of an impending attack

SUEZ CANAL AREA

CAMPAIGN IN SINAI

Egyptian Crossing / Reinforcement Phase;

Israeli Counterattacks; 6-13 October
1973

ELEVATIONS IN FEET

SCALE OF MILES

(a)

★ – Egyptian commando
attack, 6 October

Port Said

135

Attack by
repulsed 8 Oct.

Magan

Rumani

18

15

(Crossed 7 Oct)

6-7 Oct

8 Oct

Adan (-)

23

2

Ismailia

6-7 Oct

AFS GONEN

Tasa

Mendler (-)

Sharon
(Arriving 8 Oct)

16

Bir
Gifgata

21

(Crossed 11-13 Oct)

13 Oct

SECOND
THIRD

25

(Crossed 11 Oct)

4

14 (-)

(Crossed 11-13 Oct)

7

MITLA PASS

Cairo

6

19

Meron
(Arriving 9 Oct.)

Suez

40 miles

136

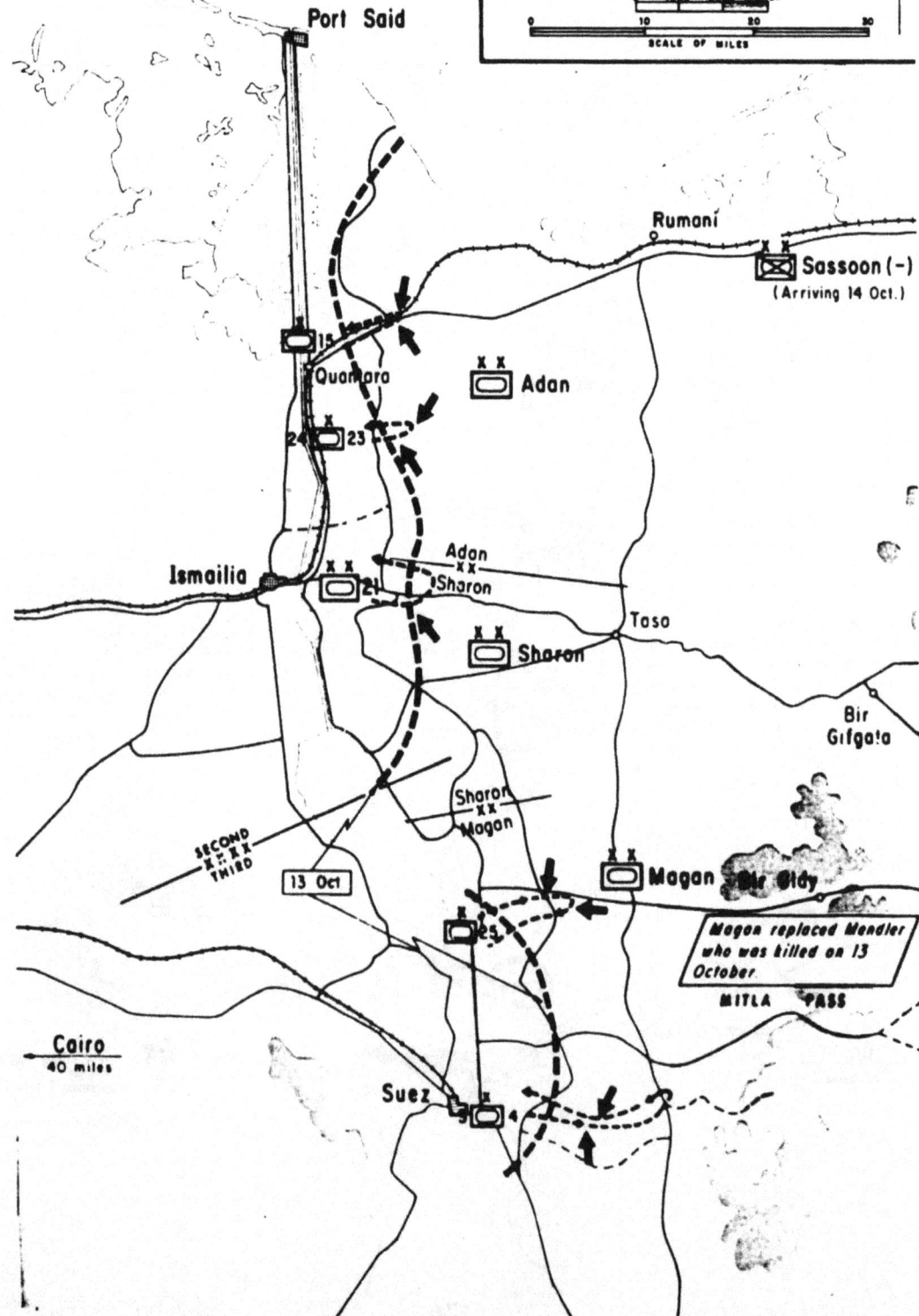

MAP II – Sinai, 14–15 October 1973

SUEZ CANAL AREA

· CAMPAIGN IN SINAI

12

Egyptian Attack, 14 October and
Israeli Counterattacks: 14-15 October
1973

b

ELEVATIONS IN FEET
1000   2000   OVER
0   10   20   30
SCALE OF MILES

MEDITERRANEAN SEA

Port Said

Rumani

Sassoon (-)
(Arriving 14 Oct.)

15
Quantara

Adan

24   23

Ismailia

21

Adan

Sharon

Taso

Sharon

Bir
Gifgata

Sharon
Magan

SECOND
THIRD

13 Oct

Magan   Bir Gidy

Magan replaced Mendler
who was killed on 13
October.

25

MITLA   PASS

Cairo
40 miles

Suez

MAP III - Sinai, 18-23 October 1973

MEDITERRANEAN SEA

SUEZ CANAL AREA
CAMPAIGN IN SINAI
OPERATION GAZELLE: Exploitation
and Isolation Egyptian Third Army,
18-23 October 1973; Egyptian Attacks

13

b

N

ELEVATIONS IN FEET
1000 2000 OVER

10   20   30

SCALE OF MILES

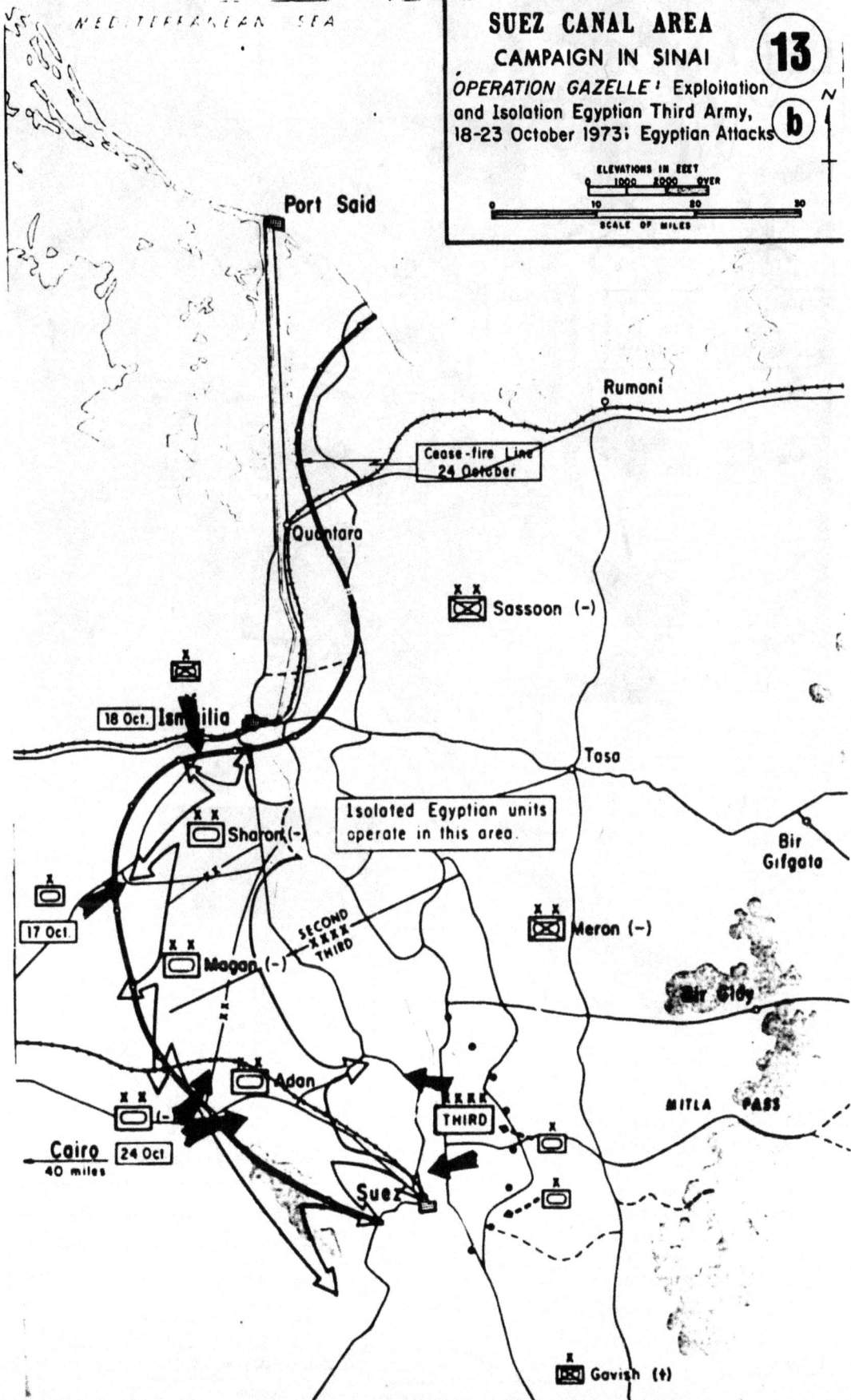

Port Said

Rumani

Cease-fire Line
24 October

Quantara

Sassoon (–)

18 Oct. Ismailia

Tasa

Sharon (–)

Isolated Egyptian units
operate in this area.

Bir
Gifgata

17 Oct

SECOND
THIRD

Meron (–)

Magan (–)

Bir Gidy

Adan

MITLA   PASS

THIRD

Cairo 24 Oct
40 miles

Suez

Gavish (†)

138

MAP IV — Golan Heights, 6-10 October 1973

LEBANON

by
...ter-borne
...orce

82

...tack in
...tack 7 Oct.

7

SYRIA

Dan

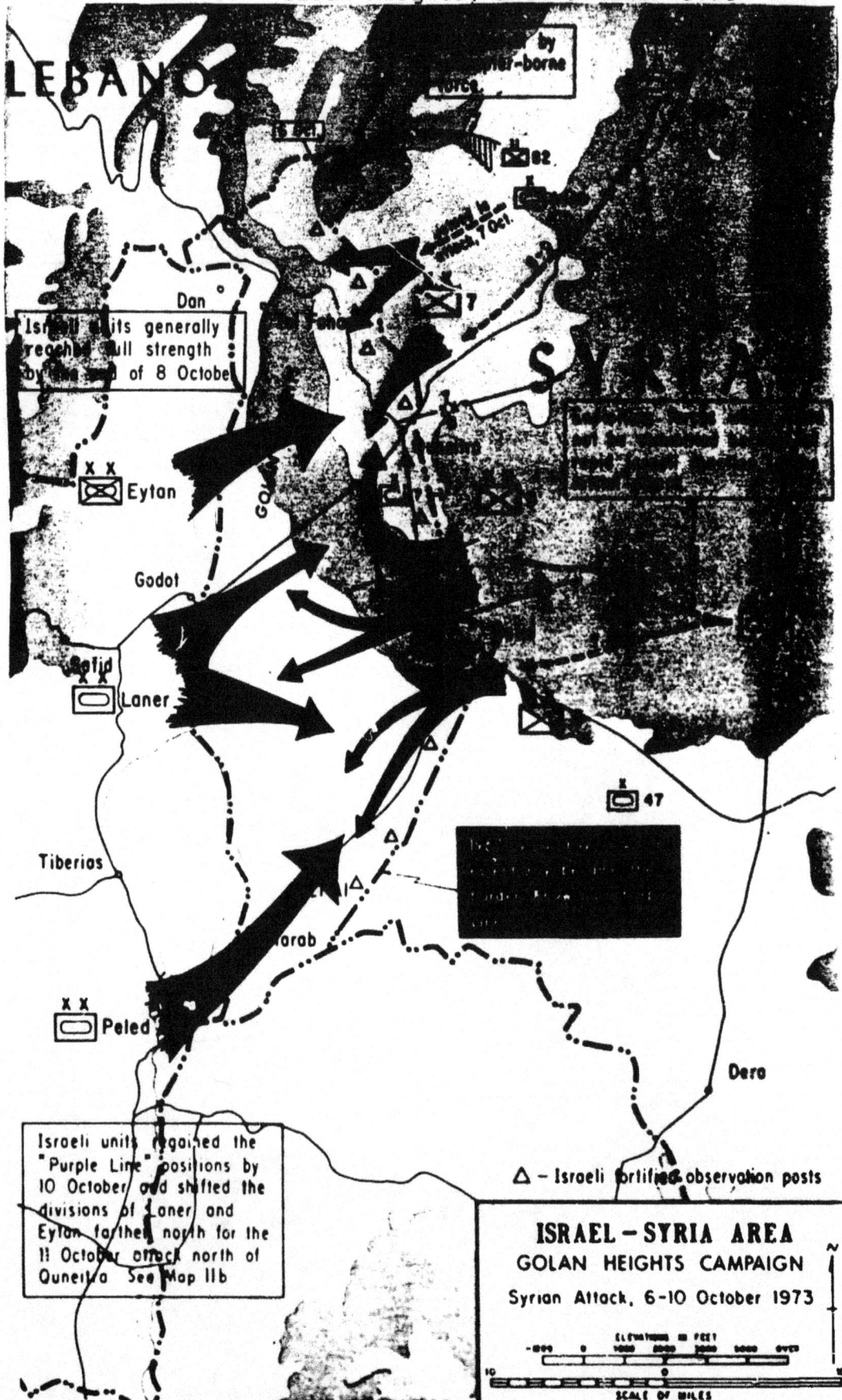

Israeli units generally
reached full strength
by the end of 8 October

X X
Eytan

Godot

47

Sofid

Laner

Tiberias

...arab

X X
Peled

Dera

Israeli units regained the
"Purple Line" positions by
10 October and shifted the
divisions of Laner and
Eytan farther north for the
11 October attack north of
Quneitra See Map IIb

△ — Israeli fortified observation posts

ISRAEL — SYRIA AREA
GOLAN HEIGHTS CAMPAIGN

Syrian Attack, 6-10 October 1973

ELEVATIONS IN FEET

SCALE OF MILES

MAP V - Golan Heights, 11-12 October 1973

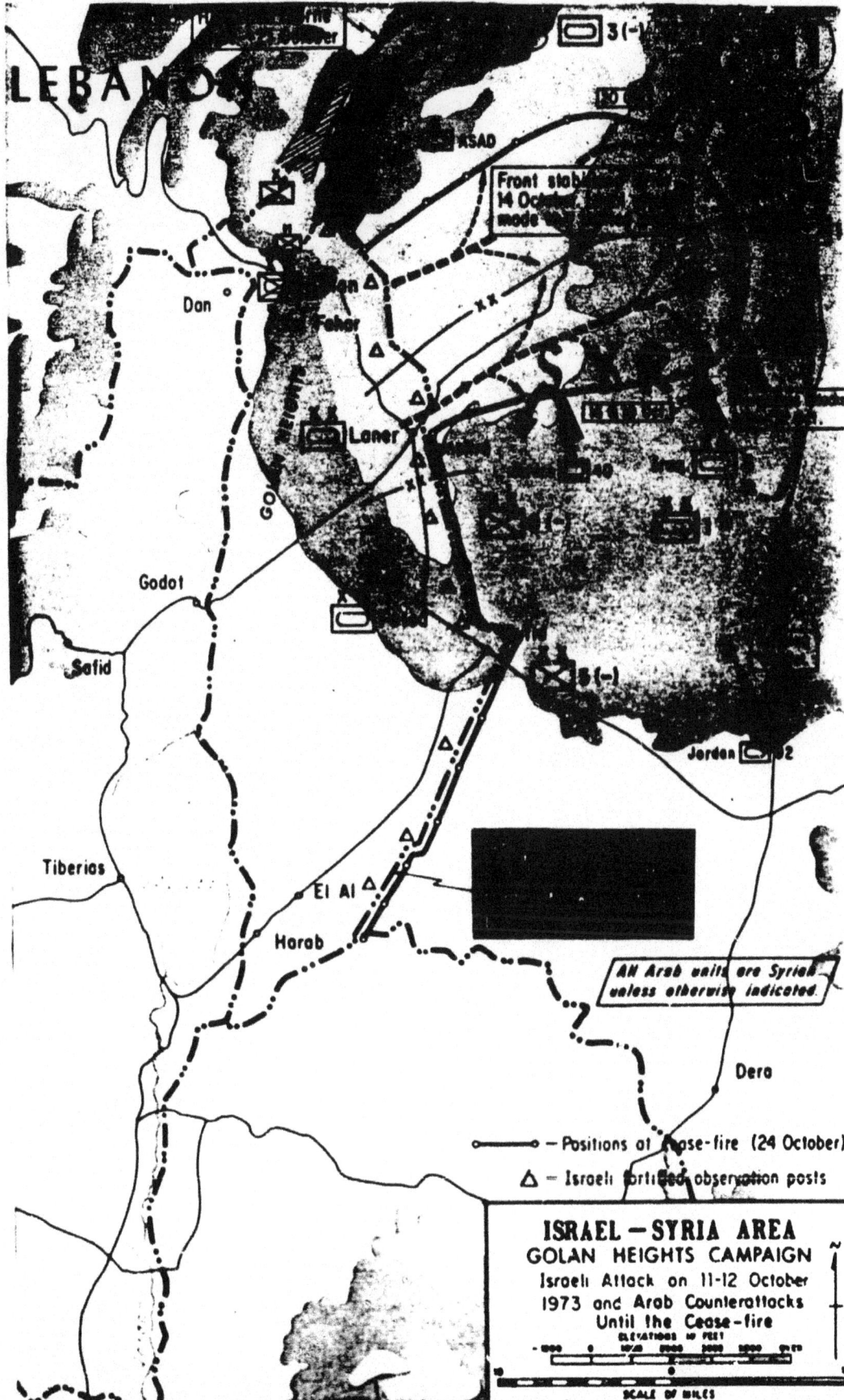

ISRAEL – SYRIA AREA
GOLAN HEIGHTS CAMPAIGN
Israeli Attack on 11-12 October
1973 and Arab Counterattacks
Until the Cease-fire

○——○ — Positions at Cease-fire (24 October)
△ — Israeli fortified observation posts

All Arab units are Syrian unless otherwise indicated.

BIBLIOGRAPHY

Bibliography

Books

Adan, Avraham. On the Banks of the Suez. Jerusalem: Edanim
    Publishers, 1979.

Aker, Frank. October 1973: The Arab-Israeli War.
    Hamden, CT: Archon Books, 1985.

Allon, Yigal. The Making of Israel's Army.
    New York: Universe Books, 1970.

Armitage, M.J. and R.A. Mason. Air Power in the
    Nuclear Age, 1945-82 Theory and Practice.
    Great Britain: Pitman Press, 1983.

Badri, Hassan EL. The Ramadan War, 1973. Cairo: United
    Company for Publishing and Distribution, 1974.

Battle, Ed L. and John R. Shea. Sensor Improvement
    for Aircraft Performing the Night/Adverse Weather
    Battlefield Interdiction Mission. Arlington,
    VA: Institute for Defense Analysis, Evaluation
    Division, June 1980.

Davis, Moshe. The Yom Kippur War. New York: Arno
    Press, 1974.

Dayan, Moshe. Moshe Dayan: Story of My Life. New York:
    William Morrow and Company, Inc., 1976.

Deitchman, Seymour J. Military Power and the Advance
    of Technology--General Purpose Military Forces for
    the 1980's and Beyond. Boulder, Colorado:
    Westview Press, 1983.

Dunnigan, James F. How to Make War--A Comprehensive Guide
    to Modern Warfare. New York: William Morrow and
    Company, 1982.

----------- and Austin Bay. A Quick & Dirty Guide To War.
    New York: William Morrow and Company, 1985.

Dupuy, T.N. The Evolution of Weapons and Warfare. New York:
  The Bobbs-Merrill Company, Inc., 1980.

----------. Elusive Victory. New York: Harper & Row,
  Publishers, Inc., 1978.

----------. Numbers, Prediction & War--Using History to
  Evaluate Combat Factors and Predict the Outcome
  of Battles. London: Macdonald   and Jane's
  Publisher's Ltd., 1979.

El-Rayyes, Riad and Dunia Nahas, ed. The October War.
  An-Nahar Arab Report Books number 3. Beirut:
  An-Nahar Press Services, 1973.

Gabriel, Richard A. Operation Peace for Galilee. Toronto:
  Collins Publishers, 1984.

Guston, Bill and Mike Spick. Modern Air Combat--Aircraft,
  Tactics and Weapons Employed in Aerial Warfare Today.
  New York: Crescent Books, 1983.

Herzog, Chiam. The Arab-Israeli Wars. New York: Random
  House, 1982.

----------. The War of Atonement, 1973. Boston:
  Little, Brown and Company, 1975.

Hotz, Robert, ed. Both Sides of the Suez--Airpower in the
  Mideast. Aviation Week & Space Technology, McGraw Hill
  Publications, 1975.

Hurley, Alfred F. and Robert C. Ehrhart. Air Power and
  Warfare. Washington D.C.: GPO, 1979.

The Insight Team of the London "Sunday Times." The Yom
  Kippur War. Garden City, N.Y.: Doubleda, . CO, 1974.

Jablonski, Edward. A Pictorial History of the Middle
  East. Garden City: Doubleday & Co., Inc., 1984.

Kahalani, Avigdor. The Heights of Courage. Westport, CT:
  Greenwood Press, 1984.

Koenig, William J. Weapons of World War 3. London: Bison
  Books Limited, 1981.

Kohler, Foy et al. The Soviet Union and the October 1973
  Middle East War. Miami: Center for Advanced
  International Studies, 1974.

The London "Sunday Times". Insight on the Middle East War.
  London: Andre Deutsch, 1974.

Luttwak, Edward N. _The Pentagon and the Art of War_. New York: Simon and Schuster, 1984.

---------- and Dan Horowitz. _The Israeli Army_. New York: Harper and Row, 1975.

Marshall, S.L.A. _Swift Sword_. New York: American Heritage Publishing Co. Inc., 1967.

Messenger, Charles. _The Blitzkrieg Story_. New York: Charles Scribner's Sons, 1976.

Military Balance 1973-1974. London: The International Institute for Strategic Studies, 1973.

Monroe, Elizabeth and A. H. Farrar-Hockley. _The Arab-Israel War, October 1973: Background and Events_. London: The International Institute for Strategic Studies, 1975. (Adelphi Papers No.111)

O'Ballance, Edgar. _No Victor, No Vanquished_. San Rafael, California: Presidio Press, 1978.

----------. _The Third Arab-Israeli War_. Hamden, CT.: The Shoestring Press, 1972.

Nordeen, Lon O. _Air Warfare in the Missile Age_. Washington D.C.: Smithsonian Institution Press, 1985.

Palit, D.K. _Return to Sinai_. New Delhi, India: Palit & Palit Publishers, 1974.

Perlmatter, Amos. _Politics and the Military in Israel 1967-77_. Totowa, NJ: Frank Cass and Company Limited, 1978.

Rothenberg, Gunther E. _The Anatomy of the Israeli Army_. NY: Hippocrene Books, Inc., 1979.

Schiff, Zeev. _October Earthquake, Yom Kippur 1973_. Translated by Louis Williams. Tel Aviv: University Publishing Projects Ltd., 1974.

---------- and Ehud Ya'ar. _Israel's Lebanon War_. New York: Simon and Schuster, 1984.

Shazly, Saad El. _The Crossing of the Suez_. San Francisco: American Mideast Research, 1980.

Sherman, Arnold. _When God Judged and Men Died_. New York: Bantam Books, 1973.

Sicherman, Harvey. The Yom Kippur War: End of Illusion.
Beverly Hills: Sage Publications, 1976.

Skinner, Michael. USAFE-A Primer of Modern Air Combat in
Europe. Novato, California: Presido Press, 1983.

Strategic Survey 1973. London: The International Institute
for Strategic Studies, 1974.

Strategic Survey 1974. London: The International Institute
for Strategic Studies, 1975.

Ulanoff, Stanley M. and David Eshel. The Fighting
Israeli Air Force. NY: Arco Publishing Inc., 1985.

Vigor, P.H. Soviet Blitzrieg Theory. New York: St.
Martin's Press, 1983.

Weizman, Ezer. On Eagles' Wings. New York: Macmillan
Publishing Co., 1977.

Whetten, Lawrence L. The Canal War. Cambridge, MA:
MIT Press, 1974.

Williams, Louis, ed. Military Aspects of the
Israeli-Arab Conflict. Tel Aviv: University
Publishing Projects, 1975.

Periodicals

"A Terrible Swift Sword." Newsweek, 21 June 1982, p. 24.

Alberts, Donald J. "A Call from the Wilderness." Air
University Review, Nov.-Dec. 1976, pp. 35-45.

Ashley, Bob. "J-SEAD: Doing It Together." Field Artillery
Journal, March-April 1985, pp. 51-53.

Barclay, C.N. "Lessons from the October War." Army,
March 1974, pp. 25-27.

Barker, A.J. "Aspects of the October 1973 War." Royal Air
Forces Quarterly, Winter 1974, pp. 301-305.

----------. "Israel the Yom Kippur War: Zagal Reflectson
the Lessons." Royal Air Forces Quarterly, Summer 1974,
pp. 28-31.

Berry, Clifton F. "USAF Doctrine Comes Alive." Air Force
Magazine, July 1983, pp. 34-36.

Brower, Kenneth S. "The Yom Kippur War." _Military Review_, March 1974, pp. 25-33.

Burns, Michael. "Tactical Air-to-Ground Weapons." _Armed Forces_, Vol.4, No.4, pp. 134-141.

Cardwell, Thomas A. "Managing Theater Air Assets." _Military Review_, May 1984, pp. 40-44.

Cobb, Tyrus W. "Tactical Air Defense--A Soviet-US Net Assessment." _Air University Review_, March-April 1979, pp. 19-38.

Coleman, Herbert J. "Israeli Air Force Decisive in War." _Aviation Week & Space Technology_, 3 Dec. 1973, pp. 18-21.

Corddry, Charles W. "The Yom Kippur War, 1973--Lessons New and Old." _National Defense_, May-June 1974, pp. 505-508.

Cordesman, Anthony H. "The NATO Central Region and the Balance of Uncertainty." _Armed Forces Journal_, July 1983, pp. 18-58.

----------. "The Sixth Arab-Israeli Conflict: Military Lessons for American Defense Planning." _Armed Forces Journal_, Aug. 1982, pp. 29-30.

Crump, Roger L. "The October War: A Postwar Assessment." _Military Review_, August 1974, pp. 12-26.

Day, Bonner. "New Role for Israeli Air Force." _Air Force Magazine_, Aug. 1978, pp. 34-39.

DeBorchgrave, Arnaud. "Israel Scores a Breakthrough." _Newsweek_, 22 October 1973, pp. 88-89.

Dupuy, T.N. "The Soviet Second Echelon: Is This a Red Herring?" _Armed Forces Journal_, Aug. 1982 pp. 60-63.

Eaker, Ira C. "Airland Battle: The Wrong Doctrine for the Wrong Reason." _Air University Review_, May-June 1985, pp. 15-22.

"Egypt Makes Major Military Shifts." _Aviation Week & Space Technology_, 17 Dec. 1973, p. 17.

Eshel, David. "Modern Inter-Arms Concepts." _Defence Update International_, No. 69, 1985, pp. 33-37.

Eshel, David et al. "The Six Day War." _Born in Battle_, No.6, pp.

4-26.

"Five Lessons of the War." Newsweek, 5 Nov. 1973, p. 54.

Forbes, Joseph and Mark Stewart. "Is Second Echelon Attack
    --A practical application of the principle of mass or a
    flawed concept with intellectually artful
    underpinnings?" Armed Forces Journal, Sept 1983, pp.
    104-106.

Gething, M. F. "Retrofit Option for USAF CAS/BAI Study."
    Defense, Sept. 1985, pp. 429-430.

Gilroy, Kevin A. "Electronic Warfare In The Air." NATO's
    Sixteen Nations, April-May 1985, pp. 58-64.

Greenhut, Jeffrey. "International Symposium on the Military
    Aspects of the Arab-Israeli Conflict." Aerospace
    Historian, Mar. 1976, pp. 21-23.

Gurion, Amnon. "Israeli Military Strategy Up to the Yom
    Kippur War." Air University Review, Sept-Oct 1982,
    pp. 52-57.

Hartman, Richard V. and Julian S. Lake. "Air Electronic
    Warfare." Proceedings, Oct. 1976, pp. 46-50.

Herzog, Chaim. "The Middle East War--A Lecture Given to
    RUSI on 6 November 1974." RUSI, Mar. 1975, pp. 3-13.

Historical Evaluation and Research Organization (HERO).
    "The Arab-Israeli October War, 1973," Combat Data
    Subscription Service, Vol. 2, No. 2, Spring 1977.

Hotz, Robert. "The Lessons of October." Aviation Week &
    Space Technology, Dec. 3 1973, p. 4.

----------. "The Mideast Surprise." Aviation Week &
    Space Technology, Oct. 15 1973, p. 7.

"Israeli Aircraft, Arab SAMs in Key Battle." Aviation Week &
    Space Technology, 22 Oct. 1974, pp. 14-17.

"Israeli F-4 Strikes on Suez Bridge Sites." Aviation Week &
    Space Technology, 31 Mar. 1975, pp. 18-19.

"Israel Scores a Breakthrough." Newsweek, 29 Oct. 1973,
    pp. 39-48.

Kantor, James C. "A-10 'Warthog' Meets All Needs for Close
    Air Support." Army Times, 25 Nov. 1985, p. 29.

Laniew, C.L. Jr. "BAI (Battlefield Air Interdiction): The

Key to the Deep Battle." _Military Review_, March 1982,
  pp. 51-54.

Ludvigsen, Eric C.   "Army-Air Force Reach Accord on Airland
  Effort." _Army_, July 1984, pp. 55-56.

Machos, James A.   "Air-land Battles or Airland Battle?"
  Military Review, July 1983.

Marshall, S.L.A.   "Tank Warrior in the Golan." _Military
  Review_, Jan. 1976, pp. 3-12.

Mayo, Charles E. "Lebanon: An Air Defense Analysis."
  Air Defense Artillery, Winter 1983, pp. 21-24.

McCabe, Richard L. "Middle East Challenges ADA Defense
  Design." _Air Defense Artillery_, Summer 1985,
  pp. 28-30.

McCoy, Tidal.   "Full Strike-The Myths and Realities
  of Airland Battle." _Armed Forces Journal_, June 1984,
  pp. 78-83.

"The Middle East Erupts." _Newsweek_, 15 Oct. 1973, pp. 38-41.

"Middle East War--October 1973." _Military Review_, Feb.
  1974, pp. 48-49.

Miller, Barry.   "Israeli Losses May Spur ECM Restudy."
  Aviation Week & Space Technology, 29 Oct.
  1973, p. 16.

-----------.   "U.S. Equips Israel with 'Smart' Guided
  Weapons." _Aviation Week & Space Technology_,
  Nov. 5 1973, p.18.

Nicolle, David.   "The Holy Day Air War." _Air Enthusiast
  International_, May 1974, pp. 240-252.

O'Ballance, Edgar.   "Some Israeli Defence Problems." _The
  Army Quarterly and Defence Journal_, Vol. 103,
  No. 2, Jan. 1973.

Peterson, Phillip A. and John R. Clark.   "Soviet Air
  and Antiair Operations." _Air University Review_,
  March-April 1985, pp. 36-54.

Power, Thomas M.   "Keepers of the Sword in the Central
  Region." _Fighter Weapons Review_, Spring 1983,
  pp. 12-16

Powers, Brian E.   "Soviet Ground Air Defense: Doctrine
  and Tactics." _Air Defense Artillery_, Summer 1985,

pp. 38-42.

Raser, Hans F. "Defense Suppression." <u>Air</u>
   <u>University</u> <u>Review</u>, July-August 1978, pp. 34-39.

Record, Jeffrey. "NATO's Forward Defense and Striking Deep."
   <u>Armed</u> <u>Forces</u> <u>Journal</u>, Nov. 1983, pp. 42-48.

Rodwell, Robert R. "The Mideast War: A Damned Close-run
   Thing." <u>Air</u> <u>Force</u> <u>Magazine</u>, Feb. 1974, pp. 36-41.

Rogers, Bernard W. "Follow-On Forces Attack(FOFA): Myths
   and Realities." <u>Parameters</u>, Summer 1985, pp. 75-79.

Ropelewski, Robert R. "Egypt Assesses Lessons of October
   War." <u>Aviation</u> <u>Week</u> <u>&</u> <u>Space</u> <u>Technology</u>, 17 Dec. 1973,
   pp. 14-17.

Roser, Hans F. "Defense Suppression." <u>Air</u>
   <u>University</u> <u>Review</u>, July-Aug. 1978, pp. 26-30.

Rosmussen, Robert D. "The Central Europe Battlefield:
   Doctrinal Implications for Counterair-Interdiction."
   <u>Air</u> <u>University</u> <u>Review</u>, July-Aug. 1978, pp. 2-20.

Safran, Nadav. "Trial By Ordeal: The Yom Kippur War,
   October 1973." <u>International</u> <u>Security</u>, Vol. 2 No. 2,
   Fall 1977, pp. 133-170.

Schemmer, Benjamin F. "NATO's New Strategy: Defend Forward,
   But Strike Deep!" <u>Armed</u> <u>Forces</u> <u>Journal</u>, Nov. 1982,
   pp. 50-68.

----------. "We Can Count On Our Allies. I'm Not Sure
   The Warsaw Pact Can Count on Theirs." <u>Armed</u> <u>Forces</u>
   <u>Journal</u>, Jan. 1982, pp. 69-70.

---------. "Will NATO's C3/EW/I Systems Let Its 'Strike
   Deep' Strategy Work?" <u>Armed</u> <u>Forces</u> <u>Journal</u>,
   Dec. 1982, pp. 92-93.

Schiff, Zeev. "The Israeli Air Force." <u>Air</u> <u>Force</u> <u>Magazine</u>,
   Aug. 1976, pp. 31-38.

Sewell, T.F. "The War of Atonement and Its Lessons." <u>The</u>
   <u>Army</u> <u>Quarterly</u> <u>and</u> <u>Defence</u> <u>Journal</u>, Vol. 106 No.1,
   Jan. 1976.

"Soviet Aid Sparks Arab Gains." <u>Aviation</u> <u>Week</u> <u>&</u> <u>Space</u>
   <u>Technology</u>, 15 Oct. 1973, pp. 12-14.

Stewart, Mark. "Second-Echelon Attack: Is the Debate
   Joined?" <u>Armed</u> <u>Forces</u> <u>Journal</u>, Sept. 1982, pp. 105-113.

Subrahmanyam, K. "The Lessons of the 1973 Arab-Israeli War." The Institute for Defence Studies and Analyses Journal, Vol. VI, Jan. 1974, pp. 416-442.

Swanson, Gregg. "Air Combat in Theory and Practice." Armed Forces Journal, Jan. 1983, pp. 33-37.

"Tactics: How the Arabs Scored Their Surprise." Newsweek, 22 Nov. 1973, pp. 85-86.

Tal, Israel. "Israel's Defense Doctrine: Background and Dynamics." Military Review, March 1978, pp. 22-37.

"The Toll: What Each Side Lost." Newsweek, 5 Nov. 1973, P. 51.

"The Two Front War." Newsweek, 22 Oct. 1973, pp. 63-82.

"U.S. Spurs Countermeasures to Israel." Aviation Week & Space Technology, 22 Oct. 1973, p. 20.

Wakebridge, Charles. "The Syrian Side of the Hill." Military Review, Feb. 1976. pp. 20-30.

----------. "A Tank Myth or a Missile Mirage." Military Review, Aug. 1976, pp. 3-11.

----------. "The Technological Gap Closes in the Middle East." National Defense, May-June 1975, pp. 460-462.

Walezk, Thomas. "October War." Strategy and Tactics, Mar.-Apr. 1977, pp. 4-18.

Walker, R.W. "Overcoming Air Defense: a misuse of airpower." Marine Corps Gazette, Oct. 1980, pp. 20-22.

"The War Nobody Won." Newsweek, 5 Nov. 1973, pp. 40-50.

Weller, Jac. "The Fight At Suez." National Defense, Sept.-Oct. 1974, pp. 130-134.

----------. "Mideast Infantry Weapons." National Defense, Mar.-Apr. 1975, pp. 371-376.

----------. "Middle East Tank Killers." RUSI, Dec. 1974, pp. 28-35.

----------. "Tanks in the Middle East." Military Review, May 1976, pp. 11-23.

Whetten, Lawrence and Michael Johnson. "Military

Lessons of the Yom Kippur War." World Today, Mar.
    1974, pp. 101-109.

Whetten, Lawrence. "War or Peace in the Middle East."
    World Today, Dec. 1974, pp. 504-512.

"Winners, Losers and Scapegoats." Newsweek, 12 Nov.
    1973, p. 54.

                        Newspapers

The New York Times.   Oct. 7-26 1973.

The Times (London).   Oct. 8-24 1973.

The Sunday Times.   Oct. 14,21,28, Nov. 4 1973.

                        Reports

Committee on Armed Services. Report of the Special
    Subcommittee on the Middle East. U.S. House and
    Senate, Washington D.C.: GPO, 1973.

Historical Evaluation and research Organization (HERO).
    Comparative Analysis Arab and Israeli Combat Performance
    1967 and 1973 Wars. McClean, VA., 1977.

Nicolai, Leland M. White Paper on the Value of
    Interdiction. Headquarters USAF/Studies and
    Analysis, Washington D.C., November 1976.

Van Creveld, Martin. Military Lessons of the Yom
    Kippur War: Historical Perspectives. The
    Center For Strategic and International Studies,
    1975.

                  Government Documents

                        Manuals

Command and General Staff College. RB 100-2 Vol. 1, The
    1973 Middle East War. Ft. Leavenworth: CGSC, 1976.

Department of the Air Force. AFM 1-1, Functions and Basic
    Doctrine of the US Air Force. Washington D.C.:
    GPO, 1984.

Department of the Army. FM 6-20, Fire Support in Combinded
    Arms Operations. Washington D.C.: GPO, 1984.

Department of the Army. FM 100-2-1, The Soviet
    Army-Operations Operations and Tactics. Washington
    D.C.: GPO, 1984.   .

Department of the Army. FM 100-2-3, The Soviet Army-Troops,
    Organization and Equipement. Washington D.C.: GPO, 1984.

Department of the Army. FM 100-5, Operations. Washington
    D.C.: GPO, 1982.

Department of the Army. FM 100-15, Corps Operations (Final
    Draft). Washington D.C.: GPO, 1985.

Department of the Army. FM 101-5-1, Operational Terms and
    Symbols(Final Draft). Washington D.C.: GPO, 1985.

Tactical Air Command Manual 2-1, Tactical Air Operations.
    Langley AFB, Virginia: Headquarters Tactical Air
    Command, 15 April 1978.

Tactical Air Command Pam. 50-26 Joint Operational Concept
    Joint Attack of the Second Echelon. Langley AFB,
    Virginia: Headquarters Tactical Air Command, 13
    December 1982.

TAC-TRADOC REDCOM, General Operating Procedures
    for Joint Attack of the Second Echelon (J-SAK), HQs
    USAF Tactical Air Command, U.S. Army Training and
    Doctrine Command, and U.S. Army Readiness Command, 31
    Dec. 1984.

                        Texts

History Department. Modern Warfare and Society Vol.II.
    Colorado Springs, CO.: USAFA, 1983.

History Department. Selected Readings in Warfare Since 1945,
West Point, N.Y.: USMA, 1981.

Military Studies Department. Professional Foundations.
    Colorado Springs, CO.: USAFA, 1983.

Military Studies Department. Airpower in Warfare.
    Colorado Springs, CO.: USAFA, 1983.

                Unpublished Material

Reports

Black, Victor L. "The Yom Kippur War: Analysis of
    Weapons Implications." China Lake, CA., July 1975.

Church, Jimmy H. and Robert T. Osterthaler. "The
    Battle for Air Superiority During the '73
    Arab-Israeli War." Quantico, VA., 7 June 1983.

Duehring, Craig W. "The A-10 and Battlefield Air
    Interdiction.(U)" Maxwell AFB, AL., April 1981.
    (SECRET)

General Research Corporation. "An Assessment of the Impact
    of the October 1973 War on Soviet Doctrine, Tactics,
    and Material." McLean, VA., July 1975. (SECRET)

Hodge, William E. et al. "Defense Suppression." Maxwell
    AFB, AL., April 1977.

Institute for Defense Analyses. "Suppression in Support
    of Offensive Air Operations.(U)"
    Arlington, VA., April 1981. (SECRET)

Jones Susan M. et al. "Historical Effects of Air
    Interdiction." McLean, VA., July 1980. (SECRET)

Kornhauser, Bernard and B.J. de Florio. "Value of
    Close Air Support." Arlington, VA., 30 June
    1976. (SECRET)

Marshall, S.L.A. "The October War--A Synopsis of the
    1973 Sinai-Suez Campaign and a Critique of Weapons and
    Tactics." Aberdeen Proving Ground, MD.,
    Jan. 1974. (SECRET)

Musella, Martin L. "Air Operations During the 1973 Arab
    Israeli War and the Implications for Marine
    Aviation." Quantico, VA., USMC Command and Staff
    College, 1985.

Office of Naval Research. "Proceedings of the
    Military Operations Research Symposium." Arlington,
    VA., July 1975. (SECRET)

Perkins, Russell G. "Comparisons of the Strategy,
    Execution, and Results of Air Warfare During the
    Middle East Conflict in 1956 and the Present
    Israel-Arab War." Washington D.C., July 1967.

Sandia Laboratories. "A Historical Analysis of the
    Effectiveness of Tactical Air Operations Against,
    and in Support of, Armored Forces." Albuquerque,

N.M., March 1981.

Special Readiness Study Group. "Lessons Learned from the 1973 Middle East Crisis." Ft. Leavenworth, KS., 28 Dec. 1973. (SECRET)

TRADOC. "31 January--12 February [1974] Visit to the Israeli Defense Forces." Ft. Monroe, VA., Mar. 1974.

TRADOC. "Analysis of Combat Data--1973 Mideast War." Ft. Monroe, VA., Aug. 1974. (SECRET)

TRADOC. "Lessons Learned from the 1973 Middle East Crisis." Ft. Monroe, VA., 11 Jan. 1974.

TRADOC. "Soviet Air Defense in the ME." Ft. Monroe, VA., 8 Jan. 1974.

U.S. Army Concepts Analysis Agency. "Middle East Game." Bethesda, MD., Jan. 1975. (SECRET)

Weapons Systems Evaluation Group. "The October 1973 Middle East War Vol. IV: Air Operations part 2." Arlington, VA., May 1975. (SECRET)

Yehuda, Borovik. "The Israeli Air Force." Wright-Patterson, AFB, Ohio, 5 Oct. 1982.

Theses

Allenback, Albert. "Tactical Airpower and the Rear Battle: Defeating the Operational Maneuver Group." Thesis, USACGSC, 1985.

Burke, David K. "A-10 Effectiveness Against Soviet Offensive Operations in Central Europe." Thesis, USACGSC, 1984.

Busico, Roger P. "Battlefield Air Interdiction: Air Power for the Future." Thesis, USACGSC, 1980.

DeMont, Robert W. and Thomas E. White. "Analysis of the Combat Empirical Tank Damage Data of the October, 1973 War." Thesis, Naval Postgraduate School, 1981.

Erickson, F.A. "The '73 War: Implications for U.S. Army Forces in NATO." Thesis, USACGSC, 1978.

Hafiz, H.H.S. "A Comparison Between US--Soviet Military Doctrine from an Egyptian Point of View." Thesis, USACGSC, 1981.

Hamilton, David. "Close Air Support and Battlefield Air
    Interdiction in the Airland Battle." Thesis,
    USACGSC, 1983.

Hayes, Donald F. "Model of a Ground Commander's Close Air
    Support Guide." Thesis, USACGSC, 1981.

Henderson, J.R. Jr. "The Air in the Airland Battle."
    Thesis, USACGSC, 1982.

Hooyer, David A. "Forward Air Control Today: Will It Work
    in Europe"? Thesis, USACGSC, 1979.

Lindsay, William E. "F-4 Phantom Aircrew Survival Equipment
    Evaluation." Thesis, USACGSC, 1979.

McClain, S.M. "Problems Associated with the Joint Air Attack
    Team." Thesis, USACGSC, 1982.

Miller, John F. "The F-16 in Offensive Air Support."
    Thesis, USACGSC, 1982.

Miller, Paul H. "The European Tactical Air Control System
    Versus Communications Jamming." Thesis, USACGSC, 1980.

Nichols, J.R. "The Joint Air Land Battle System: An
    Alternative to the Air Ground Operations System."
    Thesis, USACGSC, 1976.

Oberlin, W.C. "Analysis of USAF Close Air Support
    Training." Thesis, USACGSC, 1979.

Olschner, C.E. "The Air Superiority Battle in
    the Middle East, 1967-1973." Thesis, USACGSC, 1978.

Peterman, Robert W. "Ground Attack in the Night/Adverse
    Weather European Environment: How Do We Use the F-111
    and What Capabilities are Needed in the Future."
    Thesis, USACGSC, 1982.

Rickert, David E. "Air Superiority Concepts: 1980--2000."
    Thesis, USACGSC, 1981.

Rippe, Stephen T. "An Army and Air Force Issue: Principles
    and Procedures for Airland Warfare." Thesis,
    USACGSC, 1985.

Smith, Ross L. "CAS--Can It Survive the'80's?"
    Thesis, USACGSC, 1979.

Streater, Donald A. "Airpower Theory and Application:
    An Historical Perspective." Thesis, USACGSC, 1980.

Briefings

Smith, Fred et al. "Interdiction in Central Europe in the
    1980's--An Analysis of Forces and Capabilities." Air
    War College, Maxwell, AFB., AL., May 11 1978.

Interviews

Aklouche, Ali, CPT. Algerian Army. Personal interview.
    Nov. 17 1985.

Kadmiel, Doron, COL. Israeli Defense Force. Personal
    interview. Jan. 10 1986.

INITIAL DISTRIBUTION LIST

1. Combined Arms Research Library
   U.S. Army Command and General Staff College
   Fort Leavenworth, Kansas 66027

2. Defense Technical Information Center
   Cameron Station
   Alexandria, Virginia 22314

3. Air University Library
   Maxwell Air Force Base
   Alabama, 36112

4. LTC(P) Richard M. Swain
   ATTN: School of Advanced Military Studies
   U.S. Army Command and General Staff College
   Fort Leavenworth, Kansas 66027

5. LTC John A. Hixson
   ATTN: Combat Studies Institue
   U.S. Army Command and General Staff College
   Fort Leavenworth, Kansas 66027

6. MAJ Robert W. Peterman
   ATTN: Air Force Section
   U.S. Army Command and General Staff College
   Fort Leavenworth, Kansas 66027

www.ingramcontent.com/pod-product-compliance
Lightning Source LLC
Chambersburg PA
CBHW050354110426

42812CB00008B/2456